ISBN 978-1-332-94877-2
PIBN 10441762

1 MONTH OF
FREE
READING

at

www.ForgottenBooks.com

By purchasing this book you are eligible for one month membership to ForgottenBooks.com, giving you unlimited access to our entire collection of over 700,000 titles via our web site and mobile apps.

To claim your free month visit:

www.forgottenbooks.com/free441762

English
Français
Deutsche
Italiano
Español
Português

www.forgottenbooks.com

Mythology Photography **Fiction**
Fishing Christianity **Art** Cooking
Essays Buddhism Freemasonry
Medicine **Biology** Music **Ancient
Egypt** Evolution Carpentry Physics
Dance Geology **Mathematics** Fitness
Shakespeare **Folklore** Yoga Marketing
Confidence Immortality Biographies
Poetry **Psychology** Witchcraft
Electronics Chemistry History **Law**
Accounting **Philosophy** Anthropology
Alchemy Drama Quantum Mechanics
Atheism Sexual Health **Ancient History**
Entrepreneurship Languages Sport
Paleontology Needlework Islam
Metaphysics Investment Archaeology
Parenting Statistics Criminology
Motivational

THE

PREFACE.

AFTER extracting this detail from my Journal, and supplying many circumstances from my memory, I was very much at a lofs what title to give it. MEMOIRS feemed to anfwer my defign with the greatest propriety; but that being fo commonly mifapplied, I was afraid the public would expect a romance, where I only intended laying down a few facts, for the vindication of my own conduct. I do not, however, by this mean to fuggeft to my reader, that he will find here only a bare uninterefting narrative; no, I have added all in my power to make it ufeful and agreeable to others, as it was neceffary to myfelf; and indeed it was

highly

highly fo, fince a perfon who bears ill treatment without complaining, is generally held by his friends pufillanimous, or believed to be withheld by fecret motives from his own juftification. I know not what mine think, but it will not be amifs to inforce their good opinion of me, by laying all my actions open to their view, And as once publifhing will be more general, and fave many repetitions of a difagreeable narration, this motive firft induced me to write, to exchange my fword for a pen, that I wield as a foldier, who never dreamt of the beauties of ftile, or propriety of expreffion. Excufe then, gentle reader, all the faults that may occur, in confideration that thefe are not my weapons, and that tho' I received almoft as good an education as Virginia could beftow on me, it only fufficed to fit me for a foldier, and not for a fcholar; but tho' this was the chief end I propofed from it, I have, occafionally deviating from my main defign, added whatever I thought curious and taining, that occurred to my obfervation, in the Cherokee country, and my travels to and from it, not omitting the principal dangers

gers I have paſſed through, and the expences I have been at, that the reader, weighing them and the rewards 1 have received, may judge where the balance is due. I do not doubt but I ſhall be cenſured for expoſing ſo freely the actions of Mr. Κακοανθρωπος; but to this I was conſtrained by the clamours made againſt the unneceſſary and extravagant expences into which the reception of the Indians had drawn the government. To unveil where the unneceſſary and extravagance of it lay, became my duty; and I cannot ſay but I took ſome pleaſure in detecting the perſon in the crime he ſo arfully had laid to my charge: It is, I preſume, very pardonable in a perſon who has ſo much reaſon to complain of his unfair practices towards him. As to the manners of the Indians, I grant they have been often repreſented, and yet I have never ſeen any account to my perfect ſatisfaction, being more frequently taken from the reports of traders, as ignorant and incapable of making juſt obſervations as the natives themſelves, than from the writer's own experience. . Theſe I took upon the fpot, and if I have failed in relating them, it is thro' want of art in expreffion, and not of due knowledge in point of facts. As, however, I did not take upon me to write as an author who feeks applaufe, but compelled by the neceffity of vindicating myfelf, I once more beg the public to pafs over, with a candid indulgence, the many faults that may deferve their cenfure.

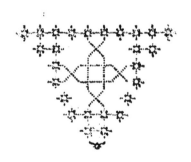

THE

THE

MEMOIRS, &c.

Otwithstanding my averfion to formal beginnings, and any thing that may relish of romance, as the reader may defire fome knowledge of the perfon who has fubmitted his actions to his judgment, I shall, in haftening to my principal defign, just acquaint him, that my father was an inhabitant of Virginia, who dying while I was yet a minor, left me a fmall fortune, no ways fufficient for my fupport, without fome employment. For fome time, by the advice of my friends, I propofed

fol-

following the more lucrative one of commerce, but after my minorſhip was elapſed, my genius burſt out. Arms had been my delight from my infancy, and I now reſolved to gratify that inclination, by entering into the ſervice. Purſuing this reſolution, I made my firſt campaign in the year 1756, with a company of gentlemen called the Patriot Blues, who ſerved the country at their own expence; but whether terrified by our formidable appearance, or ſuperior numbers, the enemy ſtill avoided us; ſo that, notwithſtanding many recent tracks and fires, we never could come to an engagement. On our return, I made application for a commiſſion in the Virginia regiment, then commanded by Col. Waſhington; but there being at that time no vacancy, I returned home.

In the year 1758, a new regiment was raiſed for that year's ſervice, to be commanded by the Hon. William Byrd, Eſq; from whom I not only received an enſigncy, but as ſubalterns were to be appointed to a troop of light-horſe,

he

he honoured me with the cornetcy of that alfo.
I was foon after ordered on an efcort, in which
fervice I continued till July, when I joined the
army at Ray's-Town, where I found General
Forbes already arrived. The army then
marched to Fort Ligonier, on the way to Fort
Du Quefne. I was feized here by a violent
fit of ficknefs, caught in fearching for fome
of the troop-horfes that were loft, by over-
heating myfelf with running, and drinking a
large quantity of cold water, which rendered
me incapable of duty. I got fomething better
about the time the troops marched for Fort Du
Quefne, and could fit my horfe when helped
on, but was ordered back by the General, who,
however, on my telling the doctor I hoped to
do duty in a day or two, permitted me to continue the march. We heard the French blow
up their magazine, while yet fome miles off;
and, on our arrival, we found the barracks,
and every thing of value, in flames. My malady rather increafed, fo that I was at laft compelled to petition for my return. I loft my horfe
at Fort Ligonier, the third I had loft during the

cam-

campaign; and being obliged to mount a very weak one, I met with great difficulty in crofsing the Allegany mountains; and before I reached Ray's Town my horfe was entirely knocked up. I bought another, and proceeded to Winchefter, where, in a little time, I got perfectly recovered.

Thofe light-horfemen that furvived the campaign, were here in want of all neceffaries; and no money being fent up from Williamf-burg to pay them, I advanced upwards of an hundred pounds, intending to reimburfe my-felf from the firft that fhould arrive; mean while the troops I belonged to were difbanded, and I, in confequence, out of pay. I had no further bufinefs at Winchefter than to wait for this money, which I did, till my patience being quite exhaufted, I refolved to go down the country in fearch of it. On my arrival at Wil-liamfburg, I was informed the money had been fent up to me by the paymafter. I returned immediately to Winchefter, near 200 miles, where I found the paymafter had paid

it

it to the Lieutenant of the troop, who had appropriated it to his own ufe. He returned me fifty pounds, but it has never been in his power to pay me the remainder, and to all appearance it never will.

After fuch unfortunate effays I began to give over all thoughts of the army, when Col. Byrd was appointed to the command of the old regiment, in the room of Col. Wafhington, who refigned; on which I was unfortunately induced to accept another commiffion. I ferved another campaign in the year 1759, under General Stanwix, in the fame quarter; but on our arrival at Pittfburg, formerly Fort Du Quefne, I had little employment, except looking over the men at work, till the fall of the leaf, when the General gave me the command of Fort Burd, about fixty miles to the eaftward of Pittfburg, where I continued about nine months at a very great expence, partly through hofpitality to thofe who paffed to and from Pittfburg, and the dearnefs of neceffaries, and partly by building myfelf a houfe,

houfe; and making feveral improvements, and finifhing the half-conftructed fort, for which I never received any gratuity. I was relieved by a company of the Penfylvania regiment in the fpring, and returned to Pittfburg, but found Col. Byrd with one half of the regiment ordered againft the Cherokees, now become our moft inveterate enemies; while the remainder under Col. Stephen were deftined to ferve on the Ohio. I will not fatigue the reader with an account of campaigns wherewith all our news-papers were filled, but confine myfelf to what more immediately concerned me.

I remained at Pittfburg till autumn, when I obtained permiffion to pafs the winter at home. I accordingly fet out in company with an Enfign named Seayres, who had obtained the fame permiffion: we found great difficulties from the badnefs of the road, of which I may quote the following inftance. After marching three whole days from Pittfburg to the place where General Braddock

firft

first croffed the Yawyawgany river (little better than fixty miles), and leaving one of my horfes faft in the mire, we found, to our great furprize, the river about twelve feet high. We waited a whole day in hopes of its falling, but had the mortification to find it had rather rofe a foot ; our provifions beginning to run fhort, we hunted to recruit them, but without any fuccefs, which obliged us to come to an immediate determination. We at laft refolved to look for fome other croffing-place ; we found about two miles lower, a part of the river, which by its breadth we judged to be fordable ; but as the water was muddy, and the bottom could not be feen, there was a confiderable rifk in attempting it, efpecially as it lay under a fall, from whence the current darted with great impetuofity. After fome deliberation, we refolved to venture it ; pufhed on by the fears of ftarving, if we remained any longer where we were, Mr. Seayres propofed himfelf to try it firft ; mounting therefore the heft of our horfes, he plunged into the ftream: for the firft hundred yards the wa-

ter

ter reached little higher than the horſe's belly, but before he got to a ſmall iſland in the middle, which we had reſolved to reſt at, he was quite up to the ſaddle-ſkirts; after halting a little time, he ſet out again for the oppoſite ſide, but found it impoſſible to proceed, a deep channel lying between him and the ſhore, into which he often plunged, but was as often obliged to turn back, at a great hazard of being carried away by the current. Deſpairing at laſt of being able to croſs it, yet unwilling to return, he forced up the ſhallow part about an hundred yards, towards the falls, making ſeveral attempts to croſs, which he at laſt effected; but the banks being exceſſively ſteep, he found as much difficulty and danger in climbing them, as he had before done in croſſing. We then followed, and tho' we now knew exactly what courſe to keep, as our horſes were weaker, and more heavily loaded, our taſk was not leſs dangerous or difficult. We found the bottom ſo rocky and irregular, that the horſes ſtaggered with their loads. The rapidity of the ſtream, and the falſe ſteps they made, threat-

threatened every moment to leave their bur-
thens and lives in the middle of the ftream.
One of them, on which my fervant was
mounted, actually fell, letting my portmantua
into the water, which luckily lodged among
the limbs of an old tree, that had been wafhed
down by the current; the horfe recovered
himfelf, and all the damage occafioned by this
accident was, the fpoiling of my cloaths, and
to the amount of forty pounds in paper money, which got fo wet, and ftuck fo faft together, that the greateft part of it was rendered
entirely ufelefs. Happy, however, that this
was our only lofs, and that we efcaped with
our lives.

In the fpring 1761, I received orders to return to my divifion, which was to proceed to
the fouthward, and join the other half againft
the Cherokees. Soon after this junction we
began our march towards the Cherokee country. Col. Byrd parted from us at a place called Stalnakres, and returned down the country, by which the command devolved on Col.

Stephen.

Stephen. We marched, without moleftation, to the great ifland on Holfton's river, about 140 miles from the enemy's fettlements, where we immediately applied ourfelves to the conftruction of a fort, which was nearly completed about the middle of November, when Kąnagatucko, the nominal king of the Cherokees, accompanied by about 400 of his people, came to our camp, fent by his countrymen to fue for peace, which was foon after granted by Col. Stephen, and finally concluded on the 19th inftant. All things being fettled to the fatisfaction of the Indians, their king told Col. Stephen he had one more favour to beg of them, which was, to fend an officer back with them to their country, as that would effectually convince the nation of the good intentions and fincerity of the Englifh towards them. The Colonel was embarraffed at the demand; he faw the neceffity of fome officer's going there, yet could not command any on fo dangerous a duty. I foon relieved him from this dilemma, by offering my fervice; my active difpofition, or, if I may venture to fay, a love

of

of my country, would not permit it's lofing
fo great an advantage, for want of refolution to
become hoftage to a people, who, tho' favage,
and unacquainted with the laws of war or
nations, feemed now tolerably fincere, and had,
feeing me employed in drawing up the articles
of peace, in a manner caft their eyes upon me
as the propereft perfon to give an account of
it to their countrymen. The Colonel feemed
more apprehenfive of the danger than I was
mvfelf, fcarce giving any encouragement to a
man whom he imagined going to make himfelf a facrifice, left he fhould incur the cenfure
of any accident that might befall me.

The 28th was fixed for our departure; but,
on making fome inquiries about our intended
journey, the Indians informed me that the rivers were, for fmall craft, navigable quite to
their country; they ftrove, however, to deter
me from thinking of that way, by laying before me the dangers and difficulties I muft en-
counter; almoft alone, in a journey fo much
further about, and continually infefted with

patiers

parties of northern Indians, who, though at peace with the Englifh, would not fail to treat, in the moſt barbarous manner, a perfon whofe errand they knew to be fo much againſt their intereſt. They profeſſed themſelves concerned for my ſafety, and intreated me to go along with them : but as I thought a thorough knowledge of the navigation would be of infinite ſervice, fhould thefe people even give us the trouble of making another campaign againſt them, I formed a refolution of going by water ; what much conduced to this, was the flownefs they march with when in a large body, and the little pleafure I could expeſt in fuch company. On the day appointed the Indians fet out on their journey, and a little after I embarked on board a canoe to purfue mine : my whole company conſiſted of a ferjeant, an interpreter, and fervant, with about ten days provifions, and to the value of twenty odd pounds in goods to buy horfes for our return : this was all our cargo, and yet we had not gone far before I perceived we were much too heavy loaded ; the canoe being fmall,

and

and very ill made, I immediately ordered my
fervant out, to join the Indians, giving him
my gun and ammunition, as we had two
others in the canoe; little could I forefee the
want we were foon to experience of them.
We then proceeded near two hundred weight
lighter, yet before we had gone a quarter of a
mile ran faft a-ground, though perhaps in the
deepeft part of the ftream, the fhoal extend-
ing quite acrofs. Sumpter the ferjeant leaped
out, and dragged us near a hundred yards over
the fhoals, till we found deep water again.
About five miles further we heard a terrible noife
of a water-fall, and it being then near night, I
began to be very apprehenfive of fome accident in paffing it: we went afhore to feek
the beft way down; after which taking out
all the falt and ammunition, left it fhould get
wet, I carried it along the fhore, while they
brought down the canoe; which they happily effected. It being now near dark, we
went afhore to * encamp about a mile below
the

* What is meant here by encamping, is only making a
fire

the fall. Here we found a party of feven or eight Cherokee hunters, of whom we made a very .particular inquiry concerning our future route : they informed us, that, had the water been high, we might from the place we then were reach their country in fix days without any impediment ; but as the water was remarkably low, by the drynefs of the preceding fummer, we fhould meet with many difficulties and dangers ; not only from the lownefs of the water, but from the northward Indians, who always hunted in thofe parts at that feafon of the year. I had already been told, and fortified myfelf againft the latter, but the former part of this talk (as they term it) no way pleafed me ; it was however too late, I thought, to look back, and fo was determined to proceed in what I had undertaken. We fupped with the Indians on diied venifon dipped in bears oil, which ferved for fauce. I lay (though I was too anxious to

fire and lying near it, though the Indians often prop a blanket or fkins upon fmall poles, to preferve them from the inclemency of the weather.

fleep)

sleep) with an Indian on a large bear-skin, and my companions, I believe, lodged much in the same manner.

Early next morning we took leave of our hosts, and in less than half an hour began to experience the troubles they had foretold us, by running a-ground; we were obliged to get out, and drag the canoe a quarter of a mile before we got off the shallow; and this was our employment two or three hours a-day, for nineteen days together, during most part of which the weather was so extremely cold, that the ice hung to our cloaths, from the time we were obliged to get in the water in the morning, till we encamped at night. This was especially disagreeable to me, as I had the courses of the river to take for upwards of two hundred and fifty miles.

We kept on in this manner, without any remarkable occurrence, till the 6th of December, when our provisions falling short, I went on shore, with the interpreter's gun, to
shoot

ſhoot a turkey ; ſingling one out, I pulled the trigger, which miſſing fire, broke off the upper chap and ſcrew-pin ; and, as I could find nei-ther, after ſeveral hours ſearch, rendered the gun unfit for ſervice. M'Cormack was not a little chagrined at the loſs of his gun ; it in-deed greatly concerned us all ; we had now but one left, and that very indifferent ; but even this we were ſhortly to be deprived of, for we were ſcarce a mile from this unlucky place, when ſeeing a large bear coming down to the water-ſide, Sumpter, to whom the remaining gun belonged, took it to ſhoot ; but not being conveniently ſeated, he laid it on the edge of the canoe, while he roſe to fix himſelf to more advantage ; but the canoe giving a heel, let the gun tumble over-board. It was irrepa-rably gone, for the water here was ſo deep, that we could not touch the bottom with our long-eſt pole. We were now in deſpair : I even deliberated whether it was not better to throw ourſelves overboard, as drowning at once ſeem-ed preferable to a lingering death. Our pro-viſions were conſumed to an ounce of meat,

and

and but very little flour, our guns loft and fpoiled, ourfelves in the heart of woods, at a feafon when neither fruit nor roots were to be found, many days journey from any habitation, and frequented only by the northern Indians, from whom we had more reafon to expect fcalping than fuccour.

We went afhore, as it was in vain to proceed, and, defponding, began to make a fire; while thus employed, feveral large bears came down a fteep hill towards us. This, at another time, would have been a joyful fight; it now only increafed our affliction. They came within the reach of a tommahawk; had we had one, and the fkill to throw it, we could fcarce have failed of killing. In fhort, they were as daring as if they had been acquainted with our misfortunes. Irritated by their bold-nefs, I formed feveral fchemes for killing, a-mong which, as mending the broken gun feemed moft probable, I inftantly fet about trying the experiment. Notching a flint on each fide, I bound it to the lower chap with a

D   leather

leather thong. This fucceeded fo far, that in ten or twelve times fnapping, it might probably fire, which was matter of great joy to us. Before I had finifhed it, the bears were frightened a-way; but as we had now mended our gun, we conceived great hopes. It was very probable they might return; and we were not long in expectation, for in lefs than a quarter of an hour, another very large one ftalked down towards us, tho' not fo near as the former ones had done. M'Cormack fnatched up his gun, and followed him near a quarter of a mile. I had fat down in expectation of the event, and pulled my fhoes and ftockings off to dry; when I heard the report of the gun, my heart leaped for joy, fince I imagined M'Cormack would have certainly taken all imaginable precautions; but judge of my defpair, when, after running myfelf out of breath, and bare-footed among the rocks and briars, I found he had miffed, and that having left the ammunition at the place where we had encamped, he could not charge again, till I returned for it. I ran back, unable as I was, and brought it; then

fat

fat down, and he continued the chace. By this time Sumpter, who had been gathering wood, joined me, and, we foon heard M'Cormack fire again; upon which, running with all our fpeed, to the place from whence the report came, we had the inexpreffible joy of feeing a large bear, that might weigh near 400 weight, weltering in his blood. It being late, we propped him for that night, on an old tree, to prevent his being devoured by other beafts. Next morning my companions fkinned him, and taking as much of his meat as we could conveniently carry, we left the camp in much better fpirits than when we came to it.

Nothing more remarkable occurred, unlefs I mark for fuch the amazing quantity of buffaloes, bears, deer, beavers, geefe, fwans, ducks, turkeys and other game, till we came to a large cave; we ftopped to examine it, but after climbing, with great difficulty, near 50 feet almoft perpendicular, to get to it, we faw nothing curious, except fome pillars of the petrified drop-

D 2

pings,

pings, that fell from the roof, of a prodigious size. I could not, indeed, penetrate very far, for want of light. Coming back to the edge of the rock, we perceived our canoe a-drift, going down with the ftream. Sumpter fcrambled down the rock, and, plunging into the river, without giving himfelf fcarce time to pull off his coat, fwam a quarter of a mile before he could overtake her. When he returned, every thing on him was ftiff frozen. We inftantly made a fire to recover him ; but this accident, joined to the feverity of the weather, obliged us to ftay the day and night following. We laid ourfelves down to fleep in the mouth of the cave, where we had made our fire, which we no fooner did, than, oppreffed with the fatigues of the preceding day, we fell into a found fleep, from which we were awaked before midnight, by the howling of wild beafts in the cave, who kept us awake with this concert till a little before day. About four o'clock in the morning, we had a more terrifying alarm, we were ftunned with a noife, like the fplitting of a rock. As there had never been, to all ap-

pear-

pearance, a fire near that place, I could no otherwife account for it, than by laying it to the fire,
which refining the air, might have occafioned
fome preffure in the cavities, or fired fome
collected vapour, the explofion of which had
been the noife that waked us ; yet, as I could
not clearly comprehend it, I was under the
greateft apprehenfions, efpecially as I could
perceive it hollow juft under us. The feverity,
however, of the weather obliged us to ftay the
next night likewife, but the howling of the
beafts, and thinking of the preceding night's
noife, prevented me from getting any fleep. On
the morning of the 9th inftant, we were, to my
great fatisfaction, obliged to decamp for want
of wood. We paffed the place where the canoe was taken up, and came to a fall about a
quarter of a mile further, which, had fhe
reached, we fhould never have feen the leaft
atom of her cargoe more.

We continued our journey much in the
fame manner till the 11th : as during the
whole time we had feen or heard nothing of
the

the northward Indians, the Cherokees had fo
menaced us with, we began to imagine ourfelves fecure, and that they had, for fome rea-
fons, impofed on us, when the report of a gun
on one fide of the river undeceived us ; for as
the Cherokees had told us how much the
northward Indians frequented this place, it
was reafonable to conclude, that they themfelves came only here to fight, at which time
they feldom fire, as that gives notice to the
enemy where to come and reconnoitre them,
but feek to hear their adverfaries fire, that their
fcouts may meafure their forces, and they take
all advantages of the enemy before they come
to action. We therefore concluded that this
muft certainly be a party of northern hunters.
We were talking of this, when another gun
from the oppofite fhore declared us in the midft
of our enemies, whom there was no refifting ;
we heard feveral more fome time after, which
made us go as far as we poffibly could before we
encamped, which we did very cautioufly, retiring
into a thicket of canes, and chufing to lay on
our wet and cold blankets, rather than make a
fire

fire to dry them, by which we might be difcovered. Next day we heard feveral more guns
on both fides of the river, which made us con-
jecture that the Indians had watched us, but
not finding our encampment the night before,
were ftill following us. I was refolved, however, to encamp in fuch an inconvenient manner no more, and to make a fire at night,
whatever might be the confequence. We
took all other imaginable precautions, encamping in a thicket of canes, impenetrable to the eye, as we had done the preceding night. About midnight fome drops
falling on my face from the trees under
which we lay, awaked me, on which I
imagined I heard fomething walk round our
camp. I lay ftill fome time to confider what
could be patroling at that time of night in the
rain, a thing unufual for wild beafts to do, when
M'Cormack, who had been awake for fome
time, afked me if I heard the noife. I told
him yes, very plain, for by the cracking of the
fticks that lay on the ground I could perceive
it approached us. M'Cormack ftarting up,

fwore

swore directly it was a party of northern Indians, and ran down, in a pannic, to the canoe, and, had not I followed to prevent him, would certainly have made off with it, and left us exposed to the mercy of the enemy, if there were any pursuing us, without any means of escape; but for my part, I imagined it some half-starved animal looking for food; and Sumpter had been so certain of this, that he never moved from where he lay; for when, in an hour after, I had persuaded M'Cormack to return to the camp, we found Sumpter fast asleep, and the noise entirely gone. We set out early the next day, on account of this alarm, and about 12 o'clock heard a noise like distant thunder. In half an hour we reached the place called the Great Falls, from which it proceeded. The river was here about half a mile broad, and the water falling from one rock to another, for the space of half a mile, had the appearance of steps, in each of which, and all about the rocks, the fish were sporting in prodigious quantities, which we might have taken with ease, had we not been too busy in working the

canoe

canoe down, to look after them. I obferved here the fame method I had with the other falls, by going afhore and looking out the fafeft way for the canoe to pafs; and left fome accident fhould happen to it, I took what falt and ammunition we had left, and carried it along the fhore : if this was not fo dangerous, it was quite as difficult a tafk ; and were I to chufe again, I fhould prefer the danger in the canoe to the difficulty of paffing fuch rocks, both hands occupied, with the care of the gun and ammunition. Theirs was no ways eafy. Before they had paffed half the fall, the canoe ran faft on a rock, and it was with the greateft difficulty they got her clear ; notwithftanding which I was at laft fo entangled among the rocks, that I was obliged to order the canoe afhore, at a place where the current was more practicable than others, and proceed in it. We fcarce advanced a hundred yards, when we ran with fuch violence againft another rock, that Sumpter, breaking his pole in attempting to ward the fhock, fell over-board ; and we narrowly efcaped being

E   par-

partakers of the fame accident. Had not the
canoe been of more than ordinary ftrength, fhe
muft certainly have dafhed to pieces; fhe
turned broadfide too, fhipping in a great deal
of water, by which all the things were wet
that I had fo much laboured to preferve. We
got out to right her; and as I obferved fome
bad places below, I refolved to wade to the
fhore, being as much an incumbrance as a
help. The water was not then above knee-
deep; but, before I reached the fhore, I got
into a fluice as high as my arm-pits, and was
near forced away by the rapidity of the ftream,
entangled in my furtout, and a blanket I had
wrapped about me : when I got on fhore, exa-
mining the damage I had fuftained, I found
my watch and papers fpoiled by the wet, and
myfelf almoft frozen; fo that, after fhivering
on three miles further, we were conftrained to
encamp, and make a fire to dry ourfelves; but
as it continued fnowing, hailing, and raining
alternately, we were again obliged to lie in
wet blankets; which, though more intolera-
ble, after the hardfhips we had fuftained this
day,

day, we had done half the time fince our departure from the Great Ifland.

Next morning, when we decamped, it was fo exceffive cold, that coming to a ftill place of the river, we found it frozen from bank to bank, to fuch a degree, that almoft the whole day was fpent in breaking the ice to make a paffage. This, indeed, had already happened fome days before, but never fo fevere as now.

Next morning we had the pleafure of finding the ice entirely gone, thawed, probably, by a hard rain that fell over-night, fo that about two o'clock we found ourfelves in Broad River, which being very high, we went the two following days at the rate of ten miles an hour, till we came within a mile of Tenneffee river, when, running under the fhore, we on a fudden difcovered a party of ten or twelve Indians, ftanding with their pieces prefented on the bank. Finding it impoffible to refift or efcape, we ran the canoe afhore towards them,

think-

thinking it more eligible to furrender immediately, which might entitle us to better treatment, than refift or fly, in either of which death feemed inevitable, from their prefented guns, or their purfuit. We now imagined our death, or, what was worfe, a miferable captivity, almoft certain, when the headman of the party agreeably furprized us, by afking, in the Cherokee language, to what town we belonged? To which our interpreter replied, To the Englifh camp; that the Englifh and Cherokees having made a peace, I was then carrying the articles to their countrymen. On this the old warrior, commonly called the Slave Catcher of Tenneffee, invited us to his camp, treated us with dried venifon, homminy, and boiled corn. He told us that he had been hunting fome time thereabouts, and had only intended returning in feven or eight days, but would now immediately accompany us.

We fet out with them next morning to purfue our voyage; but I was now obliged to give over taking the courfes of the river, left the In-

dians,

dians, who, tho' very hofpitable, are very fufpicious of things they cannot comprehend,
fhould take umbrage at it.

Entering the Teneffee River, we began to
experience the difference between going with
the ftream, and ftruggling againft it; and between eafy paddles, and the long poles with
which we were conftrained to flave, to keep
pace with the Indians, who would otherwife
have laughed at us.   When we encamped a-
bout ten miles up the river, my hands were fo
galled, that the blood trickled from them, and
when we fet out next morning I was fcarce
able to handle a pole.

Within four or five miles of the nation, the
Slave Catcher fent his wife forward by land,
partly to prepare a dinner, and partly to let me
have her place in his canoe, feeing me in pain,
and unaccuftomed to fuch hard labour, which
feat I kept till about two o'clock, when we arrived at his houfe, oppofite the mouth of Tel-
lequo river, compleating a twenty-two days
                                                  courfe

courfe of continual fatigues, hardfhips, and anxieties.

Our entertainment from thefe people was as good as the country could afford, confifting of roaft, boiled, and fried meats of feveral kinds, and very good Indian bread, baked in a very curious manner. After making a fire on the hearth-ftone, about the fize of a large difh, they fweep the embers off, laying a loaf fmooth on it; this they cover with a fort of deep difh, and renew the fire upon the whole, under which the bread bakes to as great perfection as in any European oven.

We croffed the river next morning, with fome Indians that had been vifiting in that neigbourhood, and went to Tommotly, taking Fort Loudon in the way, to examine the ruins.

We were received at Tommotly in a very kind manner by Oftenaco, the commander in chief, who told me, he had already given

me

me up for loft, as the gang I parted with at
the Great Ifland had returned about ten days
before, and that my fervant was then actually
preparing for his return, with the news of my
death.

After fmoaking and talking fome time, I delivered a letter from Colonel Stephen, and another from Captain M'Neil, with fome prefents
from each, which were gratefully accepted by
Oftenaco and his confort. He gave me a general invitation to his houfe, while I refided in
the country; and my companions found no
difficulty in getting the fame entertainment, a-
mong an hofpitable, tho' favage people, who
always pay a great regard to any one taken notice of by their chiefs.

Some days after, the headmen of each town
were affembled in the town-houfe of Chote,
the metropolis of the country, to hear the articles of peace read, whither the interpreter and
I accompanied Oftenaco.

The

The town-house, in which are tranfacted all public bufinefs and diverfions, is raifed with wood, and covered over with earth, and has all the appearance of a fmall mountain at a little diftance. It is built in the form of a fugar loaf, and large enough to contain 500 perfons, but extremely dark, having, befides the door, which is fo narrow that but one at a time can pafs, and that after much winding and turning, but one fmall aperture to let the fmoak out, which is fo ill contrived, that moft of it fettles in the roof of the houfe. Within it has the appearance of an ancient amphitheatre, the feats being raifed one above another, leaving an area in the middle, in the center of which ftands the fire; the feats of the head warriors are neareft it.

They all feemed highly fatisfied with the articles. The peace-pipe was fmoaked, and Oftenaco made an harangue to the following effect:

" The

" The bloody tommahawke, fo long lifted
" againft our brethren the Englifh, muft now
" be buried deep, deep in the ground, never to
" be raifed again *; and whoever fhall act con-
" trary to any of thefe articles, muft expect a
" punifhment equal to his offence †. Should a
" ftrict obfervance of them be neglected, a war
" muft neceffarily follow, and a fecond peace
" may not be fo eafily obtained. I therefore
" once more recommend to you, to take par-
" ticular care of your behaviour towards the
" Englifh, whom we muft now look upon as
" ourfelves; they have the French and Spa-
" niards to fight, and we enough of our own co-
" lour, without medling with either nation. I

F

defire

---

* As in this fpeech feveral allufions are made to the
cuftoms of the Indians, it may not be impertinent to acquaint the reader, that their way of declaring war, is by
fmoaking a pipe as a bond among themfelves, and lifting up
a hatchet ftained in blood, as a menace to their enemies;
at declaring peace this hatchet is buried, and a pipe fmoaked
by both parties, in token of friendfhip and reconciliation.

† The chiefs can inflict no punifhment; but, upon the
figning of the peace, it was agreed by both nations, that of-
fenders on either fide fhould be delivered up to be punifhed
by the offended party, and it is to this the Chief alludes.

" defire likewife, that the white warrior, who
" has ventured himfelf here with us, may be
" well ufed and refpected by all, wherever he
" goes amongft us."

The harrangue being finifhed, feveral pipes
were prefented me by the headfmen, to take a
whiff. This ceremony I could have waved, as
fmoaking was always very difagreeable to me;
but as it was a token of their amity, and they
might be offended if I did not comply, I put
on the beft face I was able, though I dared not
even wipe the end of the pipe that came out of
their mouths; which, confidering their paint
and dirtinefs, are not of the moft ragoutant,
as the French term it.

After fmoaking, the eatables were produced,
confifting chiefly of wild meat; fuch as venifon, bear, and buffalo; tho' I cannot much
commend their cookery, every thing being
greatly overdone: there were likewife potatoes, pumpkins, homminy, boiled corn, beans,
and peafe, ferved up in fmall flat bafkets, made

of

of fplit canes, which were diftributed amongft the croud ; and water, which, except the fpirituous liquor brought by the Europeans, is their only drink, was handed about in fmall goards. What contributed greatly to render this feaft difgufting, was eating without knives and forks, and being obliged to grope from difh to difh in the dark. After the feaft there was a dance ; but I was already fo fatigued with the ceremonies I had gone through, that I retired to Kanagatucko's hot-houfe*; but was prevented taking any repofe by the fmoke, with which I was almoft fuffocated, and the croud of Indians that came and fat on the bed-fide ; which indeed was not much calculated for repofe to any but Indians, or thofe that had paffed an apprenticefhip to their ways, as I had done: it was compofed of a few boards, fpread with bear-fkins, without any other covering ; the houfe being fo hot, that I could not endure the weight of my own blanket.

F 2   Some

* This Hot-Houfe is a little hut joined to the houfe, in which a fire is continually kept, and the heat fo great, that cloaths are not to be borne the coldeft day in winter.

Some hours after I got up to go away, but met Oftenaco, followed by two or three Indians, with an invitation from the headman of Settico, to vifit him the next day.

I fet out with Oftenaco and my interpreter in the morning, and marched towards Settico, till we were met by a meffenger, about half a mile from the town, who came to ftop us till every thing was prepared for our reception: from this place I could take a view of the town, where I obferved two ftand of colours flying, one at the top, and the other at the door of the town-houfe; they were as large as a fheet, and white. Left therefore I fhould take them for French, they took great care to inform me, that their cuftom was to hoift red colours as an emblem of war; but white, as a token of peace. By this time we were joined by another meffenger, who defired us to move forward.

About 100 yards from the town-houfe we were received by a body of between three and

four

four hundred Indians, ten or twelve of which were entirely naked, except a piece of cloth about their middle, and painted all over in a hideous manner, fix of them with eagles tails in their hands, which they fhook and flourifhed as they advanced, danced in a very uncommon figure, finging in concert with fome drums of their own make, and thofe of the late unfortunate Capt. Damere; with feveral other inftruments, uncouth beyond defcription. Cheulah, the headman of the town, led the proceffion, painted blood-red, except his face, which was half black, holding an old rufty broad-fword in his right hand, and an eagle's tail in his left. As they approached, Cheulah, fingling himfelf out from the reft, cut two or three capers, as a fignal to the other eagle-tails, who inftantly followed his example. This violent exercife, accompanied by the band of mufick, and a loud yell from the mob, lafted about a minute, when the headman waving his fword over my head, ftruck it into the ground, about two inches from my left foot; then directing himfelf to
me,

me, made a short discourse (which my interpreter told me was only to bid me a hearty
welcome) and presented me with a string of
beads. We then proceeded to the door, where
Cheulah, and one of the beloved men, taking me by each arm, led me in, and seated
me in one of the first seats; it was so dark
that nothing was perceptible till a fresh supply
of canes were brought, which being burnt in
the middle of the house answers both purposes of fuel and candle. I then discovered a-
bout five hundred faces; and Cheulah addres-
sing me a second time, made a speech much
to the same effect as the former, congratulating
me on my safe arrival thro' the numerous parties
of the northern Indians, that generally haunt
the way I came. He then made some profes-
sions of friendship, concluding with giving me
another string of beads, as a token of it.
He had scarce finished, when four of those
who had exhibited at the procession made their
second appearance, painted milk-white, their
eagle-tails in one hand, and small goards with
beads in them in the other, which they rat-
tled

tled in time to the mufick. During this dance the peace-pipe was prepared ; the bowl of it was of red ftone, curioufly cut with a knife, it being very foft, tho' extremely pretty when polifhed. Some of thefe are of black ftone, and fome of the fame earth they make their pots with, but beautifully diverfified. The ftem is about three feet long, finely adorned with porcupine quills, dyed feathers, deers hair, and fuch like gaudy trifles.

After I had performed my part with this, I was almoft fuffocated with the pipes prefented me on every hand, which I dared not to decline. They might amount to about 170 or 180; which made me fo fick, that I could not ftir for feveral hours.

The Indians entertained me with another dance, at which I was detained till about feven o'clock next morning, when I was conducted to the houfe of Chucatah, then fecond in command, to take fome refrefhment. Here I found a white woman, named Mary Hughes,
who

who told me fhe had been prifoner there near
a twelvemonth, and that there ftill remained a-
mong the Indians near thirty white prifoners
more, in a very miferable condition for want of
cloaths, the winter being particularly fevere ;
and their mifery was not a little heightened by
the ufage they received from the Indians. I
ordered her to come to me to Oftenaco's, with
her miferable companions, where I would dif-
tribute fome fhirts and blankets I had brought
with me amongft them, which fhe did fome
days after.

After a fhort nap, I arofe and went to the
town-houfe, where I found the chiefs in con-
fultation; after fome time, I was called upon,
and defired to write a letter for them to the
Governor of South Carolina, which fignified
their defire of living in peace with the Englifh,
as long as the fun fhone, or grafs grew, and
defired that a trade might be opened between
them. Thefe wrote, I fealed them up, with
fome wampum and beads in the infide. I
was the fame day invited to Chilhowey,
where

where I was received and treated much in the same manner as at Settico. I wrote some letters; and one that Yachtino the headman had brought from Col. Stephen was interpreted to them, which seemed to give them great satisfaction. I found here a white man, who, notwithstanding the war, lived many years among them ; he told me that the lower towns had been greatly distressed when attacked by Colonel Montgomery ; being obliged to live many months upon horse-flesh, and roots out of the woods, occasioned partly by the numbers drove among them, and the badness of the crops that year.

Returning home with Ostenaco the next day, being the 2d of January 1762, I enquired whether he thought I should receive any more invitations ? He told me he believed not, because the towns to which I had already been invited, having been our most inveterate enemies during the war, had done this, as an acknowledgment and reparation of their fault.

G   I had

I had now leifure to complete taking the courfes of the river, from which, as I have already mentioned, I was deterred by the Indians, as likewife to make remarks upon the country and inhabitants.

The country being fituated between thirty-two and thirty-four degrees north latitude, and eighty-feven degrees thirty minutes weft longitude from London, as near as can be calculated, is temperate, inclining to heat during the fummer-feafon, and fo remarkably fertile, that the women alone do all the laborious tafks of agriculture, the foil requiring only a little ftirring with a hoe, to produce whatever is required of it; yielding vaft quantities of peafe, beans, potatoes, cabbages, Indian corn, pumpions, melons, and tobacco, not to mention a number of other vegetables imported from Europe, not fo generally known amongft them, which flourifh as much, or more here, than in their native climate; and, by the daily experience of the goodnefs of the foil, we

may

may conclude, that, with due care, all European plants might fucceed in the fame manner.

Before the arrival of the Europeans, the natives were not fo well provided, maize, melons, and tobacco, being the only things they beftow culture upon, and perhaps feldom on the latter. The meadows or favannahs produce excellent grafs ; being watered by abundance of fine rivers, and brooks well ftored with fifh, otters and beavers ; having as yet no nets, the Indians catch the fifh with lines, fpears, or dams; which laft, as it feems particular to the natives of America, I fhall trouble the reader with a defcription of. Building two walls obliquely down the river from either fhore, juft as they are near joining, a paffage is left to a deep well or refervoir ; the Indians then fcaring the fifh down the river, clofe the mouth of the refervoir with a large bufh, or bundle made on purpofe, and it is no difficult matter to take them with bafkets, when inclofed within fo fmall a compafs.

North

North America, being one continual foreſt, admits of no ſcarcity of timber for every uſe; there are oaks of ſeveral ſorts, birch, aſh, pines, and a number of other trees, many of which are unknown in Europe, but already deſcribed by many authors. The woods like-wiſe abound with fruits and flowers, to which the Indians pay little regard. Of the fruits there are ſome of an excellent flavour, particu-larly ſeveral ſorts of grapes, which, with pro-per culture, would probably afford an excel-lent wine. There are likewiſe plumbs, cher-ries, and berries of ſeveral kinds, ſomething different from thoſe of Europe; but their peaches and pears grow only by culture: add to theſe ſeveral kinds of roots, and medicinal plants, particularly the plant ſo eſteemed by the Chineſe, and by them called gingſang, and a root which never fails curing the moſt inve-terate venereal diſeaſe, which, however, they never had occaſion for, for that diſtemper, be-fore the arrival of Europeans among them. There are likewiſe an incredible number of buffaloes, bears, deer, panthers, wolves, foxes,

racoons,

racoons, and opoffums. The buffaloes, and moft of the reft, have been fo often defcribed, and are fo well known, that a defcription of them would be but tedious; the opoffum, however, deferves fome attention, as I have never feen it properly defcribed. It is about the fize of a large cat, fhort and thick, and of a filver colour. It brings forth its young; contrary to all other animals, at the teat, from whence, when of a certain fize, and able to walk, it drops off, and goes into a falfe belly, defigned by providence in its dam for its reception, which, at the approach of danger, will, notwithftanding this additional load, climb rocks and trees with great agility for its fecurity.

There are a vaft number of leffer fort of game, fuch as rabbits, fquirrels of feveral forts, and many other animals; befide turkeys, geefe, ducks of feveral kinds, partridges, pheafants, and an infinity of other birds, purfued only by the children, who, at eight or ten years old, are very expert at killing with a farbacan,

bacan, or hollow cane, through which they
blow a small dart, whose weaknefs obliges
them to fhoot at the eye of the larger fort of
prey, which they feldom mifs.

There are likewife a great number of rep-
tiles, particularly the copper-fnake, whofe bite
is very difficult to cure, and the rattle-fnake,
once the terror of Europeans; now no longer
apprehended, the bite being fo eafily cured ;
but neither this, nor any other fpecies, will attempt biting unlefs difturbed or trod upon ;
neither are there any animals in America mif-
chievous unlefs attacked. The flefh of the
rattle-fnake is extremely good; being once
obliged to eat one through want of provifions,
I have eat feveral fince thro' choice.

Of infects, the flying ftag is almoft the only
one worthy of notice ; it is about the fhape of
a beetle, but has very large beautiful branching
horns, like thofe of a ftag, from whence it
took its name.

The

The Indians have now a numerous breed of horses, as also hogs, and other of our animals, but neither cows nor sheep; both these, however, might be supplied by breeding some tame buffaloes, from which, I have been informed, some white prisoners among them have procured both butter and cheese; and the fine long shag on its back could supply all the purposes of wool.

The mountains contain very rich mines of gold, silver, lead, and copper, as may be evinced by several accidentally found out by the Indians, and the lumps of valuable ore washed down by several of the streams, a bag of which sold in Virginia at a considerable price; and by the many salt springs, it is probable there are many mines of that likewise, as well as of other minerals. The fountains too may have many virtues, that require more skilful persons than the Cherokees or my self to find out.

They have many beautiful stones of different colours, many of which, I am apt to believe,

lieve, are of great value ; but their fuperftition has always prevented their difpofing of them to the traders, who have made many attempts to that purpofe ; but as they ufe them in their conjuring ceremonies, they believe their parting with them, or bringing them from home, would prejudice their health or affairs. Among others, there is one in the poffeffion of a conjurer, remarkable for its brilliancy and beauty, but more fo for the extraordinary manner in which it was found. It grew, if we may credit the Indians, on the head of a monftrous ferpent, whofe retreat was, by its brilliancy, difcovered ; but a great number of fnakes attending him, he being, as I fuppofe by his diadem, of a fuperior rank among the ferpents, made it dangerous to attack him. Many were the attempts made by the Indians, but all fruftrated, till a fellow, more bold than the reft, cafing himfelf in leather, impenetrable to the bite of the ferpent or his guards, and watching a convenient opportunity, furprifed and killed him, tearing this jewel from his head, which the conjurer has kept hid for many

years,

years, in some place unknown to all but two women, who have been offered large presents to betray it, but steadily refused, lest some signal judgment or mischance should follow. That such a stone exists, I believe, having seen many of great beauty; but I cannot think it would answer all the encomiums the Indians bestow upon it. The conjurer, I suppose, hatched the account of its discovery; I have however given it to the reader, as a specimen of an Indian story, many of which are much more surprising.

The Cherokees are of a middle stature, of an olive colour, tho' generally painted, and their skins stained with gun-powder, pricked into it in very pretty figures. The hair of their head is shaved, tho' many of the old people have it plucked out by the roots, except a patch on the hinder part of the head, about twice the bigness of a crown-piece, which is ornamented with beads, feathers, wampum, stained deers hair, and such like baubles. The ears are slit and stretched to an enormous size,

H   putting

putting the perfon who undergoes the operation to incredible pain, being unable to lie on either fide for near forty days. To remedy this, they generally flit but one at a time ; fo foon as the patient can bear it, they are wound round with wire to expand them, and are adorned with filver pendants and rings, which they likewife wear at the nofe. This cuftom does not belong originally to the Cherokees, but taken by them from the Shawnefe, or other northern nations.

They that can afford it wear a collar of wampum, which are beads cut out of clamfhells, a filver breaft-plate, and bracelets on their arms and wrifts of the fame metal, a bit of cloth over their private parts, a fhirt of the Englifh make, a fort of cloth-boots, and mockafons, which are fhoes of a make peculiar to the Americans, ornamented with porcupine-quills ; a large mantle or match-coat thrown over all compleats their drefs at home.; but when they go to war they. leave their trinkets behind, and the mere neceffaries ferve them.

The

The women wear the hair of their head, which is ſo long that it generally reaches to the middle of their legs, and ſometimes to the ground, club'd, and ornamented with ribbons of various colours; but, except their eyebrows, pluck it from all the other parts of the body, eſpecially the looſer part of the ſex. The reſt of their dreſs is now become very much like the European; and, indeed, that of the men is greatly altered. The old people ſtill remember and praiſe the ancient days, before they were acquainted with the whites, when they had but little dreſs, except a bit of ſkin about their middles, mockaſons, a mantle of buffalo ſkin for the winter, and a lighter one of feathers for the ſummer. The women, particularly the half-breed, are remarkably well featured; and both men and women are ſtreight and well-built, with ſmall hands and feet.

The warlike arms uſed by the Cherokees are guns, bows and arrows, darts, ſcalp-

ping-

ping-knives, and tommahawkes, which, are
hatchets; the hammer-part of which being
made hollow, and a small hole running from
thence along the shank, terminated by a small
brass-tube for the mouth, makes a compleat
pipe. There are various ways of making these,
according to the country or fancy of the pur-
chafer, being all made by the Europeans;
some have a long spear at top, and some different conveniencies on each side. This is one
of their most useful pieces of field-furniture,
serving all the offices of hatchet, pipe, and
sword; neither are the Indians less expert at
throwing it than using it near, but will kill at
a considerable distance.

They are of a very gentle and amicable dif-
position to those they think their friends, but
as implacable in their enmity, their revenge
being only compleated in the entire destruction
of their enemies. They were pretty hospita-
ble to all white strangers, till the Europeans
encouraged them to scalp; but the great reward offered has led them often since to commit

mit as great barbarities on us, as they formerly only treated their moſt inveterate enemies
with. They are very hardy, bearing heat,
cold, hunger and thirſt, in a ſurprizing manner; and yet no people are given to more ex-
ceſs in eating and drinking, when it is conveniently in their power: the follies, nay miſ-
chief, they commit when inebriated, are entirely laid to the liquor; and no one will revenge any injury (murder excepted) received
from one who is no more himſelf: they are
not leſs addicted to gaming than drinking, and
will even loſe the ſhirt off their back, rather
than give over play, when luck runs againſt
them.

They are extremely proud, deſpiſing the lower claſs of Europeans; and in ſome athletick
diverſions I once was preſent at, they refuſed
to match or hold conference with any but
officers.

Here, however, the vulgar notion of the
Indians uncommon activity was contradicted
by

by three officers of the Virginia regiment, the
floweft of which could outrun the fwifteft
of about 700 Indians that were in the place
but had the race exceeded two or three hundred
yards, the Indians would then have acquired
the advantage, by being able to keep the fame
pace a long time together; and running being
likewife more general among them, a body of
them would always greatly exceed an equal
number of our troops.

They are particularly careful of the fuper-
annuated, but are not fo till of a great age;
of which Oftenaco's mother is an inftance.
Oftenaco is about fixty years of age, and the
youngeft of four; yet his mother ftill conti-
nues her laborious tafks, and has yet ftrength
enough to carry 200 weight of wood on her
back near a couple of miles. I am apt to
think fome of them, by their own computa-
tion, are near 150 years old.

They have many of them a good unculti-
vated genius, are fond of fpeaking well, as that

paves

paves the way to power in their councils; and
I doubt not but the reader will find some
beauties in the harangues I have given him,
which I affure him are entirely genuine. Their
language is not unpleafant, but vaftly afpirated,
and the accents fo many and various, you
would often imagine them finging in their
common difcourfe.   As the ideas of the Che
rokees are fo few, I cannot fay much for the
copioufnefs of their language.

They feldom turn their eyes on the perfon
they fpeak of, or addrefs themfelves to, and
are always fufpicious when people's eyes are
fixed upon them.   They fpeak fo low, except in council, that they are often obliged to
repeat what they were faying; yet fhould a
perfon talk to any of them above their common pitch, they would immediately afk him,
if he thought they were deaf?

They have likewife a fort of loofe poetry, as
the war-fongs, love-fongs, &c.   Of the latter many contain no more than that the young
'man

man loves the young woman, and will be uneafy, according to their own expreffion, if he
does not obtain her. Of the former I fhall prefent the following fpecimen, without the original in Cherokee, on account of the expletive
fyllables, merely introduced for the mufic, and
not the fenfe, juft like the toldederols of many
old Englifh fongs.

A Translation of the WAR SONG.

Caw waw noo dee, &c.

WHERE'ER the earth's enlighten'd by the fun,
    Moon fhines by night, grafs grows, or wa-
    ters run,
Be't known that we are going, like men, afar,
In hoftile fields to wage deftructive war;
Like men we go, to meet our country's foes,
Who, woman-like, fhall fly our dreaded blows;
Yes, as a woman, who beholds a fnake,
In gaudy horror, gliften thro' the brake,
Starts trembling back, and ftares with wild furprize,
Or pale thro' fear, unconfcious, panting, flies.
* Juft fo thefe foes, more tim'rous than the hind,
Shall leave their arms and only cloaths behind;

Pinch'd

* As the Indians fight naked, the vanquifhed are conftrained

Pinch'd by each blaſt, by ev'ry thicket torn,
Run back to their own nation, now its ſcorn:
Or in the winter, when the barren wood
Denies their gnawing entrails nature's food,
Let them ſit down, from friends and country far,
And wiſh, with tears, they ne'er had come to war.

   * We'll leave our clubs, dew'd with their coun-
      try ſhow'rs,
And, if they dare to bring them back to our's,
Their painted ſcalps ſhall be a ſtep to fame,
And grace our own and glorious country's name.
Or if we warriors ſpare the yielding foe,
Torments at home the wretch muſt undergo †.

                          But

ſtrained to endure the rigours of the weather in their
flight, and live upon roots and fruit, as they throw down
their arms to accelerate their flight thro' the woods.

   * It is the cuſtom of the Indians, to leave a club, ſomething of the form of a cricket-bat, but with their warlike
exploits engraved on it, in their enemy's country, and the
enemy accepts the defiance, by bringing this back to their
country.

   † The priſoners of war are generally tortured by the
women, at the party's return, to revenge the death of thoſe
that have periſhed by the wretch's countrymen. This

                  ſavage

But when we go, who knows which fhall return,
When growing dangers rife with each new morn?
Farewel, ye little ones, ye tender wives,
For you alone we would conferve our lives!
But ceafe to mourn, 'tis unavailing pain,
If not fore-doom'd, we foon fhall meet again.
But, O ye friends! in cafe your comrades fall,
Think that on you our deaths for vengeance call;
With uprais'd tommahawkes purfue our blood,
And ftain, with hoftile ftreams, the confcious wood,
That pointing enemies may never tell
The boafted place where we, their victims, fell *

Both

favage cuftom has been fo much mitigated of late, that the
prifoners were only compelled to marry, and then generally allowed all the privileges of the natives. This lenity,
however, has been a detriment to the nation; for many of
thefe returning to their countrymen, have made them acquainted with the country-paffes, weaknefs, and haunts of
the Cherokees; befides that it gave the enemy greater cou-
rage to fight againft them.

* Their cuftom is generally to engrave their victory on
fome neighbouring tree, or fet up fome token of it near
the field of battle; to this their enemies are here fuppofed
to point to, as boafting their victory over them, and the
flaughter that they made.

Both the ideas and verfe are very loofe in the original, and they are fet to as loofe a mufic, many compofing both tunes and fong off hand, according to the occafion; tho' fome tunes, efpecially thofe taken from the northern Indians, are extremely pretty, and very like the Scotch.

The Indians being all foldiers, mechanifm can make but little progrefs; befides this, they labour under the difadvantage of having neither proper tools, or perfons to teach the ufe of thofe they have: Thus, for want of faws, they are obliged to cut a large tree on each fide, with great labour, to make a very clumfy board; whereas a pair of fawyers would divide the fame tree into eight or ten in much lefs time: confidering this difadvantage, their modern houfes are tolerably well built. A number of thick pofts is fixed in the ground, according to the plan and dimenfions of the houfe, which rarely exceeds fixteen feet in breadth, on account of the roofing, but often extend to fixty or feventy in length, befide the

I 2   little

little hot-houfe. Between each of thefe pofts is placed a fmaller one, and the whole wattled with twigs like a bafket, which is then covered with clay very fmooth, and fometimes white-wafhed. Inftead of tiles, they cover them with narrow boards. Some of thefe houfes are two ftory high, tolerably pretty and capacious ; but moft of them very inconvenient for want of chimneys, a fmall hole being all the vent affigned in many for the fmoak to get out at.

Their canoes are the next work of any confequence ; they are generally made of a large pine or poplar, from thirty to forty feet long, and about two broad, with flat bottoms and fides, and both ends alike ; the Indians hollow them now with the tools they get from the Europeans, but formerly did it by fire : they are capable of carrying about fifteen or twenty men, are very light, and can by the Indians, fo great is their fkill in managing them, be forced up a very ftrong current, particularly

ticularly the bark canoes ; but thefe are feldom uſed but by the northern Indians.

They have of late many tools among them,
and, with a little inſtruction, would foon become proficients in the uſe of them, being
great imitators of any thing they fee done ;
and the curious manner in which they drefs
ſkins, point arrows, make earthen veffels,
and baſket-work, are proofs of their inge-
nuity, poffeffing them a long time before the
arrival of Europeans among them. Their
method of pointing arrows is as follows :
Cutting a bit of thin braſs, copper, bone, or
fcales of a particular fifh, into a point with
two beards, or fome into an acute triangle,
they fplit a little of their arrow, which is generally of reeds ; into this they put the point,
winding fome deers finew round the arrow,
and through a little hole they make in the
head ; then they moiften the finew with their
fpittle, which, when dry, remains faft glewed,
nor ever untwiſts. Their bows are of feveral
forts of wood, dipped in bears oil, and feafoned
before

before the fire, and a twifted bear's gut for the
ftring.

They have two forts of clay, red and white,
with both which they make excellent veffels,
fome of which will ftand the greateft heat.
They have now learnt to few, and the men
as well as women, excepting fhirts, make all
their own cloaths; the women, likewife, make
very pretty belts, and collars of beads and
wampum, alfo belts and garters of worfted.
In arts, however, as in war, they are greatly
excelled by their northern neighbours.

Their chief trade is with thofe Europeans
with whom they are in alliance, in hides, furs,
&c. which they barter by the pound, for all other
goods; by that means fupplying the deficiency
of money. But no proportion is kept to their
value; what coft two fhillings in England,
and what coft two pence, are often fold for
the fame price; befides that, no attention is
paid to the goodnefs, and a knife of the beft
temper and workmanfhip will only fell for the

fame

fame price as an ordinary one. The reafon of this is, that, in the beginning of the commerce, the Indians finding themfelves greatly impofed upon, fixed a price on each article, according to their own judgment; powder, balls, and feveral other goods, are by this means fet fo low, that few people would bring them, but that the Indians refufe to trade with any perfon who has not brought a proportionable quantity, and the traders are cautious of lofing a trade in which 5 or 600 per cent. in many articles fully recompences their lofs in thefe.

As to religion, every one is at liberty to think for himfelf; whence flows a diverfity of opinions amongft thofe that do think, but the major part do not give themfelves that trouble. They generally concur, however, in the belief of one fuperior Being, who made them, and governs all things, and are therefore never difcontent at any misfortune, becaufe they fay, the Man above would have it fo. They believe in a reward and punifhment, as may be evinced by their anfwer to Mr. Martin, who,

who, having preached fcripture till both his
audience and he were heartily tired, was told
at laft, that they knew very well, that, if they
were good, they fhould go up; if bad, down;
that he could tell no more; that he had long
plagued them with what they no ways under
ftood, and that they defired him to depart the
country. This, probably, was at the inftigation
of their conjurers, to whom thefe people pay
a profound regard; as chriftianity was entirely
oppofite, and would foon difpoffefs the people
of their implicit belief in their juggling art,
which the profeffors have brought to fo great
perfection as to deceive Europeans, much
more an ignorant race, whofe ideas will naturally augment the extraordinary of any thing
the leaft above their comprehenfion, or out of
the common tract. After this I need not fay
that in every particular they are extremely fu-
perftitious, that and ignorance going always
hand in hand.

They have few religious ceremonies, or
ftated times of general worfhip: the green

corn

corn dance feems to be the principal, which
is, as I have been told, performed in a very
folemn manner, in a large fquare before the
town-houfe door: the motion here is very
flow, and the fong in which they offer thanks
to God for the corn he has fent them, far
from unpleafing. There is no kind of rites
or ceremonies at marriage, courtfhip and all
being, as I have already obferved, concluded
in half an hour, without any other celebra-
tion, and it is as little binding as ceremonious;
for though many laft till death, efpecially
when there are children, it is common for a
perfon to change three or four times a-year.
Notwithftanding this, the Indian women gave
lately a proof of fidelity, not to be equalled
by politer ladies, bound by all the facred ties
of marriage.

Many of the foldiers in the garrifon of
Fort Loudoun, having Indian wives, thefe
brought them a daily fupply of provifions,
though blocked up, in order to be ftarved to
a furrender, by their own countrymen; and

K   they

they perfifted in this, notwithftanding the exprefs orders of Willinawaw, who, fenfible of
the retardment this occafioned, threatened
death to thofe who would affift their enemy ;
but they laughing at his threats, boldly told
him, they would fuccour their hufbands every
day, and were fûre, that, if he killed them,
their relations would make his death atone
for theirs. Willinawaw was too fenfible of
this to put his threats into execution, fo that
the garrifon fubfifted a long time on the provifions brought to them in this manner.

When they part, the children go with, and
are provided for, by the mother. As foon as
a child is born, which is generally without
help, it is dipped into cold water and wafhed,
which is repeated every morning for two
years afterward, by which the children acquire
fuch ftrength, that no ricketty or deformed
are found amongft them. When the woman
recovers, which is at lateft in three days, fhe
carries it herfelf to the river to wafh it ; but
though three days is the longeft time of their
illnefs,

illnefs, a great number of them are not fo many hours ; nay, I have known a woman delivered at the fide of a river, wafh her child, and come home with it in one hand, and a goard full of water in the other.

They feldom bury their dead, but throw them into the river; yet if any white man will bury them, he is generally rewarded with a blanket, befides what he takes from the corpfe, the dead having commonly their guns, tommahawkes, powder, lead, filver ware, wampum, and a little tobacco, buried with them ; and as the perfons who brings the corpfe to the place of burial, immediately leave it, he is at liberty to difpofe of all as he pleafes, but muft take care never to be found out, as no-thing belonging to the dead is to be kept, but every thing at his deceafe deftroyed, except thefe articles, which are deftined to accompa-ny him to the other world. It is reckoned, therefore, the worft of thefts; yet there is no punifhment for this, or any other crime, mur-

der

der excepted, which is more properly revenged than puni∫hed.

This cu∫tom was probably introduced to prevent avarice, and, by preventing hereditary acqui∫itions, make merit the ∫oie means of acquiring power, honour, and riches. The inventor, however, had too great a knowledge of the human mind, and our propen∫ity to po∫∫e∫s, not to ∫ee that a ∫uperior pa∫∫ion mu∫t intercede; he therefore wi∫ely made it a religious ceremony, that ∫uper∫tition, the ∫tronge∫t pa∫∫ion of the ignorant, might check avarice, and keep it in the bounds he had pre∫cribed. It is not known from whence it came, but it is of great antiquity, and not only general over all North America, but in many parts of A∫ia. On this account the wives generally have ∫eparate property, that no inconveniency may a-ri∫e from death or ∫eparation.

The Indians have a particular method of relieving the poor, which I ∫hall rank among the mo∫t laudable of their religious ceremonies,

mo∫t

moſt of the reſt conſiſting purely in the vain
ceremonies, and ſuperſtitious romances of their
conjurors.   When any of their people are
hungry, as they term it, or in diſtreſs, orders
are iſſued out by the headmen for a war-dance,
at which all the fighting men and warriors aſ-
ſemble; but here, contrary to all their other
dances, one only dances at a time, who, after
hopping and capering for near a minute, with
a tommahawke in his hand, gives a ſmall hoop,
at which ſignal the muſic ſtops till he relates
the manner of taking his firſt ſcalp, and con-
cludes his narration, by throwing on a large
ſkin ſpread for that purpoſe, a ſtring of wampum, piece of plate, wire, paint, lead, or any
thing he can moſt conveniently ſpare ; after
which the muſic ſtrikes up, and he proceeds
in the ſame manner through all his warlike
actions: then another takes his place, and the
ceremony laſts till all the warriors and fighting men have related their exploits.   The
ſtock thus raiſed, after paying the muſicians,
is divided among the poor.   The ſame ceremony is made uſe of to recompence any extraordinary

traordinary merit. This is touching vanity in a tender part, and is an admirable method of making even imperfections conduce to the good of fociety.

Their government, if I may call it government, which has neither laws or power to fupport it, is a mixed ariftocracy and democracy, the chiefs being chofe according to their merit in war, or policy at home; thefe lead the warriors that chufe to go, for there is no laws or compulfion on thofe that refufe to follow, or punifhment to thofe that forfake their chief: he ftrives, therefore, to infpire them with a fort of enthufiafm, by the war-fong, as the ancient bards did once in Britain Thefe chiefs, or headmen, likewife compofe the affemblies of the nation, into which the war-women are admitted. The reader will not be a little furprifed to find the ftory of Amazons not fo great a fable as we imagined, many of the Indian women being as famous in war, as powerful in the council.

The

The reft of the people are divided into two military claffes, warriors and fighting men, which laft are the plebeians, who have not diftinguifhed themfelves enough to be admitted into the rank of warriors. There are fome other honorary titles among them, conferred in reward of great actions ; the firft of which is Outacity, or Man-killer ; and the fecond Colona, or the Raven. Old warriors likewife, or war-women, who can no longer go to war, but have diftinguifhed themfelves in their younger days, have the title of Beloved. This is the only title females can enjoy; but it abundantly recompences them, by the power they acquire by it, which is fo great, that they can, by the wave of a fwan's wing, deliver a wretch condemned by the council, and already tied to the ftake.

Their common names are given them by their parents ; but this they can either change, or take another when they think proper; fo that fome of them have near half a dozen, which the Englifh generally increafe, by giving

an

an Englifh one, from fome circumftance in their
lives or difpofition, as the Little Carpenter to
Attakullakulla, from his excelling in building
houfes; Judd's friend, or corruptly the Judge,
to Oftenaco, for faving a man of that name
from the fury of his countrymen; or fometimes a tranflation of his Cherokee name, as
Pigeon to Woey, that being the fignification
of the word. The Over-hill fettlement is by
thefe two chiefs divided into two factions, between whom there is often great animofity,
and the two leaders are fure to oppofe one another in every meafure taken. Attakullakulla
has done but little in war to recommend him,
but has often fignalized himfelf by his policy,
and negotiations at home. Oftenaco has a tolerable fhare of both; but policy and art are
the greateft fteps to power. Attakullakulla
has a large faction with this alone, while
Oconneftoto, fir-named the Great Warrior, famous for having, in all his expeditions, taken fuch prudent meafures as never to have
loft a man, has not fo much power, and
Oftenaco could never have obtained the fuperiority,

periority, if he had not a great reputation in both.

On my arrival in the Cherokee country, I found the nation much attached to the French, who have the prudence, by familiar politeneſs, (which coſts but little, and often does a great deal) and conforming themſelves to their ways and temper, to conciliate the inclinations of almoſt all the Indians they are acquainted with, while the pride of our officers often diſguſts them; nay, they did not ſcruple to own to me, that it was the trade alone that induced them to make peace with us, and not any preference to the French, whom they loved a great deal better. As however they might expect to haſten the opening of the trade by telling me this, I ſhould have paid but little regard to it, had not my own obſervations confirmed me, that it was not only their general opinion, but the policy of moſt of their head-men; except Attakullakulla, who conſerves his attachment inviolably to the Engliſh.

L

I ſhall

I shall be accused, perhaps, for mentioning policy among so barbarous a nation; but tho' I own their views are not so clear and refined as those of European statesmen, their alliance with the French seems equal, proportioning the lights of savages and Europeans, to our most masterly strokes of policy; and yet we cannot be surprized at it, when we consider that merit alone creates their ministers, and not the prejudices of party, which often create ours.

The English are now so nigh, and encroached daily so far upon them, that they not only felt the bad effects of it in their hunting grounds, which were spoiled, but had all the reason in the world to apprehend being swallowed up, by so potent neighbours, or driven from the country, inhabited by their fathers, in which they were born, and brought up, in fine, their native soil, for which all men have a particular tenderness and affection. The French lay farther off, and were not so powerful; from them, therefore, they had less to fear.

fear. The keeping thefe foreigners then more upon a footing, as a check upon one another, was providing for their own fafety, and that of all America, fince they forefaw, or the French took care to fbew them, that, fhould they be driven out, the Englifh would in time extend themfelves over all North America. The Indians cannot, from the woods of America, fee the true ftate of Europe: report is all they have to judge by, and that often comes from perfons too interefted to give a juft account. France s circumftances were not in fuch a flourifhing condition as was reprefented; the French were conquered, and a war carried into the heart of the Cherokee country; many of their towns were facked and plundered without a poffibility of relieving them, as they lay ftraggled on a large extent of ground, many miles from one another; it was then their intereft, orrather they were compelled, to afk for peace and trade, without which they could no longer flourifh.

Were

Were arts introduced, and the Cherokees contracted into a fortified settlement, governed by laws, and remoter from the English, they might become formidable; but hunting must be then laid more aside, and tame cattle supply the deficiency of the wild, as the greater the number of hunters, the more prey would be required; and the more a place is haunted by men, the less it is resorted to by game. Means might be taken, would the Cherokees follow them, to render the nation considerable; but who would seek to live by labour, who can live by amusement? The sole occupations of an Indian life, are hunting, and warring abroad, and lazying at home. Want is said to be the mother of industry, but their wants are supplied at an easier rate.

Some days after my reception at Chilhowey, I had an opportunity of seeing some more of their diversions. Two letters I received from some officers at the Great Island occasioned a great assembly at Chote, where I was conduct-ed to read them; but the Indians finding nothing

thing that regarded them, the greater part
refolved to amufe themfelves at a game they
call nettecawaw; which I can give no o-
ther defcription of, than that each player having a pole about ten feet long, with feveral
marks or divifions, one of them bowls a round
ftone, with one flat fide, and the other convex,
on which the players all dart their poles after
it, and the neareft counts according to the
vicinity of the bowl to the marks on his pole.

'As I was informed there was to be a phyfic-
dance at night, curiofity led me to the town-
houfe, to fee the preparation. A veffel of their
own make, that might contain twenty gallons
(there being a great many to take the medicine) was fet on the fire, round which ftood
feveral goards filled with river-water, which
was poured into the pot; this done, there
arofe one of the beloved women, who, opening
a deer-fkin filled with various roots and herbs,
took out a fmall handful of fomething like fine
falt; part of which fhe threw on the headman's
feat, and part into the fire clofe to the pot; fhe
                                        then

then took out the wing of a fwan, and after flourifhing it over the pot, ftood fixed for near a minute, muttering fomething to herfelf; then taking a fhrub-like laurel (which I fuppof-ed was the phyfic) fhe threw it into the pot, and returned to her former feat. As no more ceremony feemed to be going forward, I took a walk till the Indians affembled to take it. At my return I found the houfe quite full: they danced near an hour round the pot, till one of them, with a fmall goard that might hold about a gill, took fome of the phyfic, and drank it, after which all the reft took in turn. One of their headmen prefented me with fome, and in a manner compelled me to drink, though I would have willingly declined. It was however much more pa-latable than I expected, having a ftrong tafte of faffafras: the Indian who prefented it, told me it was taken to wafh away their fins; fo that this is a fpiritual medicine, and might be ranked among their religious ceremonies. They are very folicitous about its fuccefs; the conjurer, for feveral mornings before it is

drank

drank, makes a dreadful howling, yelling, and hallowing, from the top of the town-houfe, to frighten away apparitions and evil fpirits. According to our ideas of evil fpirits, fuch hideous noifes would by fympathy call up fuch horrible beings; but I am apt to think with the Indians, that fuch noifes are fufficient to frighten any being away but themfelves.

I was almoft every night at fome dance, or diverfion; the war-dance, however, gave me the greateft fatisfaction, as in that I had an opportunity of learning their methods of war, and a hiftory of their warlike actions, many of which are both amufing and inftructive.

I was not a little pleafed likewife with their ball-plays (in which they fhew great dexterity) efpecially when the women played, who pulled one another about, to the no fmall amufement of an European fpectator.

They

They are likewife very dexterous at panto-
mime dances; feveral of which I have feen performed that were very diverting. In one of
thefe, two men, dreffed in bear-fkins, came in,
ftalking and pawing about with all the motions
of real bears: two hunters followed them, who
in dumb fhew acted in all refpects as they would
do in the wood: after many attempts to fhoot
them, the hunters fire; one of the bears is
killed, and the other wounded; but, as they
attempt to cut his throat, he rifes up again, and
the fcuffle between the huntfmen and the
wounded bear generally affords the company a
great deal of diverfion.

The taking the pigeons at rooft was another
that pleafed me exceedingly; and thefe, with
my walking and obfervations, furnifhed me
with amufement for fome time; but the feafon
not always permitting my going abroad, and
as I had fo little to do at home, I foon grew
tired of the country. The Indian fenate indeed
would fometimes employ me in reading and
writing letters for them; of which I generally

acquitted

acquitted myfelf to their fatisfaction, by adding what I thought would be acceptable, and retrenching whatever might difpleafe.

On the 17th, a party came home from hunting on Holfton's River, bringing with them an eagle's tail, which was celebrated at night by a grand war-dance, and the perfon who killed it had the fecond war-title of Colona conferred upon him, befides the bounty gathered at the war-dance, in wampum, fkins, &c. to the amount of thirty pounds; the tail of an eagle being held in the greateft efteem, as they fometimes are given with the wampum in their treaties, and none of their warlike ceremonies can be performed without them.

This Indian acquainted the headman of a current report in the Englifh camp, that a large body of Englifh were to march next fpring through the Cherokees country, againft the French. There was little probability or poffibility in fuch a report, yet it was received with fome degree of belief; every thing of

M   news,

news, every flying rumour, is fwallowed here
by the populace. The leaft probability is exaggerated into a fact, and an Indian from our
camp, who fcarce underftands four or five
words of a converfation between two common foldiers, who often know as little of
the ftate of affairs as the Indians themfelves,
turn all the reft of it to fomething he fufpects,
and imagines he has heard what was never once
mentioned; and this, when he returns to his
own country, is paffed about as a certainty.
From hence flows the continual miftakes the
Indians unavoidably make in their councils ;
they muft act according to intelligence, and it
requires a great penetration indeed to difcern the
truth, when blended with fo much falfity:
thus they are often obliged to act according
to the report of a miftaken or lying Indian,
who are all but too much adicted to this
vice, which proved a continual fund of uneafinefs to me all the time I remained in their
country.

On

On the 26th of January, advices were received from the Great Ifland, that fome Cherokees had been killed by the northern Indians, who had been encouraged, and much careffed, by the commanding officer. This piece of news feemed greatly to difpleafe them; they fufpended however their judgment, till further intelligence. I began to be very uneafy for the return of an exprefs I had fent out on my arrival, who was to come back by the Great Ifland, and was the only perfon who could give me any accounts I could rely on, as I was fenfible the Indian one was infinitely exaggerated. We were yet talking of this, when the *News Hallow* was given from the top of Tommotly town-houfe; whereupon Oftenaco rofe from the table, and went immediately to the town-houfe, where he ftaid till day. On afking him next morning, What news? he feemed very unwilling to tell me, and went out of the houfe, feemingly very much difpleafed. I then made the fame queftion to feveral other Indians, whofe different ftories convinced me it was fomething they endeavoured to conceal.

I was

I was under fome apprehenfion at this unufual incivility. It was no wonder I was alarm-
ed; had the Englifh given any encouragement
to thefe northern ravagers, nay, had the French
faction perfuaded their countrymen of our coun-
tenancing them in the flaughter, the meaneft of
the deceafed's relations had it in his power to
facrifice me to their manes, and would certainly have done it, fince, in default of kindred,
their revenge falls on any of the fame country
that unfortunately comes within their reach;
and nothing could be a protection to an hoftage,
when capitulating could not fave the garrifon of
Fort Loudoun : a body of Indians purfued
them, and breaking through the articles, and
all the laws of war and humanity, furprifed
and butchered them. Difguifing, however,
my uneafinefs, I feemingly took to fome diverfions, while I fent M'Cormack to pry into the
true caufe of fuch a change ; he following my
hoft, found no difficulty in fhuffling amongft
the crowd into the town-houfe, where Oftenaco made the following fpeech.

" We

" We have had fome bad talks lately from
" the Great Ifland, which I hope neverthelefs
" are not true, as I fhould be very forry that
the peace, fo lately concluded with our bre-
" thren the Englifh, fhould be broke in fo
" fhort a time : we muft not judge as yet of
" what we have heard from the Great Ifland.
" If Bench the exprefs does not return foon, I
" myfelf will raife a party, and go to the Great
" Ifland, where I fhall get certain information
" of all that has happened."

This fpeech was received with fhouts of applaufe, and the affembly betook themfelves to
dancing.

On the 28th, I was invited to a grand eagle's
tail dance, at which about 600 perfons of both
fexes were affembled. About midnight, in
the heat of their diverfion, news was brought
of the death of one of their principal men,
killed at the Great Ifland by the northern Indians. This put a fudden ftop to their diverfion, and nothing was heard but threats of
ven-

vengeance. I eafily concluded that this could only proceed from the confirmation of the ill news already received. I tried as much as laid in my power to mollify their anger, by telling them, that, if any accident had happened to their people, it was neither by confent or approbation of the Englifh; that tho' the northern Indians were our allies as well as they, I was certain more favour would be fhewn them than their enemies, as Capt. M Neil, who commanded the fort, was a good, humane, brave officer, and had always fhewn fo much friendfhip for their nation, as to leave no room to doubt of his protection to any of their people who fhould be under his care. This fatisfied them fo well, that fome propofed dancing again; but as it was late, they agreed to give over their diverfion for that night.

On the 4th of February, an account came in almoft contradictory to this. An Indian woman from Holfton's River was the meffenger, who related, that the northern Indians had turned their arms againft the Englifh, and

were

were then actually building a breaſt-work within a quarter of a mile of Fort Robinſon ; that, whilſt one half were employed in carrying on the work, the other obſerved the motions of our people ; but this lie was even too groſs for Indians to digeſt ; tho' the next day, another who came in confirmed it, and moreover affirmed the enemy's fortifications to be already breaſt-high.

The 15th was the day appointed for the return of the Little Carpenter ; and his not arriving began to give his friends a great deal of uneaſineſs. Oſtenaco bore likewiſe his ſhare in it, as his brother was of the party. Here is a leſſon to Europe ; two Indian chiefs, whom we call barbarians, rivals of power, heads of two oppoſite factions, warm in oppoſing one another, as their intereſt continually claſh ; yet theſe have no farther animoſity, no family-quarrels or reſentment, and the brother of the chief who had gained the ſuperiority is a volunteer under his rival's command.

For

For my part, I was no lefs anxious about the exprefs. I difpatched my fervant out to meet him, and bring me the particulars of what had been tranfacted at the Great Ifland ; he return-ed in about five or fix days, with the letters the exprefs had been charged with, leaving him to make out the reft of the journey as his fatigue would permit. Among others was a letter from Capt. M'Neil, informing me, that a par-ty of about feventy northern Indians came to Fort Robinfon a fhort time after I had left it, who told him, that they came from Pittfburg, with a pafs from the commanding officer, to join us againft the Cherokees, not knowing that we had already concluded a peace. They feemed very much diffatisfied at coming fo far to no purpofe, and demanded if any Cherokees were near? They were anfwered, that a party were out a hunting ; but, if they would be looked upon as friends to the Englifh, they muft not meddle with them, while under the pro-tection of the commanding officer. The Indi-ans, however, paying but little regard to this admonition, went immediately in purfuit of
them,

them, and finding them a few hours after, as in no apprehension of any enemy, they fired on them before they discovered themselves, killing one, and wounding another, who however made his escape to the fort. His countrymen all did the same, without returning the fire, as few of their guns were loaded, and they inferior in number Their enemies pursued them to the fort, but could never see them after, as Capt. M'Neil took great care to keep them asunder. Finding therefore no more likelihood of scalping, the northern Indians marched away from the fort.

This was the same party I encamped with the first night after my departure from the Great Island, and were surprised at the same place, where they had still continued.

He farther informed me, that I should probably find Fort Robinson, and all the posts on the communication, evacuated, as the regiment was to be broke.

N   1 made

I made this letter public, with which they
feemed tolerably well fatisfied, particularly
when I feigned the wounded Indian was under
the care of an Englifh furgeon, who would not
fail to cure him in a little time.

I now began to be very defirous of returning, and acquainted Oftenaco of my anxiety,
defiring him to appoint fifteen or twenty headmen, agreeable to the orders I had received
from Col. Stephen, as likewife to collect all
the white perfons and negroes, to be fent con-
formable to the articles of peace, to Fort
Prince-George. He replied, that, as foon as
the white prifoners returned from hunting,
where they then were with their mafters (the
white people becoming flaves, and the property of thofe that take them) he would fet about
the performance. Some time after this, when
all the prifoners were come in, I again attacked
Oftenaco; but then his horfes could not be
found, and there was a neceffity of having one
or two to carry my baggage and his own. I
then waited till the horfes were found; but
when

I fuppofed all things ready for our departure, I was greatly furprifed to find it delayed. Oftenaco told me, that one of the Carpenter's party, which was on its return home, had come in the night before, and reported, that the Carolinians had renewed the war before they had well concluded a peace. The Indian had, according to cuftom, a long account of it; but tho' I fhewed the improbability of fuch a ftory, Oftenaco refufed to fet out before the Carpenter arrived, which was not till the 23d following. He brought in the fame report, but owned he did not believe it, as it was told him by a perfon who he thought wanted to raife fome difturbance.

I now began to be very prefling with Oftenaco, threatening if he would not fet out immediately, to return without him. This however would have been my laft refource, as I was for the fpace of 140 miles ignorant of every ftep of the way. I at laft prevailed on him; but on the 10th of March, while we were again preparing for our departure, the *Death*

Hallow

Hallow was heard from the top of Tommotly town-houſe. This was to give notice of the return of a party commanded by Willinawaw, who went to war towards the Shawneſe country ſome time after my arrival. After ſo many diſappointments, I began to think I ſhould never get away, as I ſuppoſed this affair would keep me, as others had done, two or three days, and till ſome new accident ſhould intervene to detain me longer. About eleven o'clock the Indians, about forty in number, appeared within ſight of the town ; as they approached, I obſerved four ſcalps, painted red on the fleſh-ſide, hanging on a pole, and carried in front of the line, by the ſecond in command, while Willinawaw brought up the rear. When near the town-houſe, the whole marched round it three times, ſinging the war-ſong, and at intervals giving the *Death Hallow* ; after which, ſticking the pole juſt by the door, for the crowd to gaze on, they went in to relate in what manner they had gained them. Curioſity prompted me to follow them into the town-houſe ; where,

after

after smoaking a quarter of an hour in silence, the chief gave the following account of their campaign.

" After we left Tommotly, which was about
" the middle of ˙ January, we travelled near
" 400 miles before we saw the least sign of the
" enemy ; at last, one evening, near the river
" Ohio, ·we heard the report of several guns,
" whereupon I sent out several scouts to disco-
" ver who they were, and if possible where they
" encamped, that we might attack them early
" next morning ; about dark the scouts returned,
" and informed us they were a party of Shaw-
" nese, hunting buffaloes ; that they had
" watched them to the river-side, where, taking
" to their canoes, they had paddled across the
" river ; and seeing a great many fires on the
" other side, where our scouts directed our
" sight, we concluded it to be a large emcamp-
" ment ; we thereupon began to consult, whe-
" ther it would be more adviseable to crofs the
" river over-night, or early next morning: it was
" de-

(94)

"decided in favour of the former, notwith-
"standing its snowing excessively hard, lest we
"should be discovered. We accordingly strip-
"ped ourselves, tying our guns to our backs,
"with the buts upwards, to which we hung
"our ammunition, to prevent its getting wet;
"we then took water, and swam near half a
"mile to the other side, where we huddled to-
"gether to keep ourselves warm, intending
"to pass the remainder of the night in that
"manner, and to fall on the enemy at day-
"break; but as it continued snowing the whole
"time, it proved so cold, that we could endure
"it no longer than a little past midnight, when
"we resolved to surround the enemy's camp,
"giving the first fire, and, without charging
"again, run on them with our tommahawkes,
"which we had tucked in our belts for that pur-
"pose, should there be occasion. We accor-
"dingly surrounded them; but when the sig-
"nal was given for firing, scarce one fourth of
"our guns went off, wet with the snow, not-
"withstanding all the precautions we had ta-
"ken

ken to preferve them dry : we then rufhed
" in ; but, before we came to a clofe engage-
" ment, the enemy returned our fire ; as, it was
" at random, not being able to fee us before we
" were upon them, on account of the darknefs
" of the night, and the thicknefs of the bufhes,
" we received no damage. They had not time
" to charge again, but fought us with the buts
" of their guns, tommahawkes, and firebrands.
" In the beginning of the battle we took two
" prifoners, who were continually calling out to
" their countrymen to fight ftrong, and they
" would foon conquer us ; this made them
" fight much bolder, till the perfons who had
" the prifoners in cuftody put a ftop to it, by
" finking a tommahawke in each of their fkulls,
" on which their countrymen took to flight,
" and left every thing behind them. As foon
" as it was day, we examined the field, where
" we found two more of the enemy dead, one
" of which was a French warrior, which, with
" the prifoners we had killed, are the four
" fcalps we have brought in. We loft only
" one

" one man, the poor brave Raven of Togua,
" who ran rafhly before us in the midft of the
" enemy. We took what things we could
" conveniently bring with us, and deftroyed the
" reft."

Having finifhed his account of the expedi-
tion, out of his fhot-pouch he pulled a piece
of paper, wrapped up in a bit of birch-bark,
which he had taken out of the Frenchman's
pocket, and gave it to me to look at, afking
if I did not think it was his commiffion? I replied in the negative, telling him it was only
fome private marks of his own, which I did not
underftand. It appears to me to have been his
journal, every feventh line being longer than the
others, to denote the Sunday ; the death's head,
and other maiks, relate to what happened on
the feveral days ; but having filled his paper long
before his death, he had fupplied it by inter-
lining with a pin. Thefe are my conjectures,
I have however annexed it here from the original,

ginal, ftill in my poffeffion, that each reader
may make his own.

About one o'clock the baggage and all things
being ready, Oftenaco took leave of his friends,
tho' this ceremony is unufual among them, and
we began our march fooner than I expected.
Paffing thro' Toqua, we faw feveral Indians
weeping for the death of their relations, killed
in the late battle. In an hour's time we arrived
at Chote, where we found a great number of
headmen affembled to give us a talk, contain-
ing inftructions to my Indian conductors, to re-
mind the Englifh of their promifes of friendfhip, and to prefs the Governor of Virginia to
open a trade; for the Indians to behave well to
the inhabitants when they arrived, as that was the
only way to keep the chain of friendfhip bright;
that we fhould keep a good look-out, as the e-
nemy were very numerous on the path. What
occafioned this precaution, and probably Oftenaco's delaying his departure fo long, was, the
defeat of a party of about thirty Indians, who
went out to war fome time before, the fame way

that

that we were to go, eight of whom had been killed or taken. They attributed this lofs to the want of arrows, the northern Indians having poured feveral vollies of arrows, and done great execution, before the Cherokees could charge again, after the firft fire. This was efpecially difadvantageous to the Cherokees, as both parties met unexpectedly on the top of a mountain, which they were both croffing, and engaged fo clofe, that the northern Indians availed themfelves of this advantage, and the fuperiority of their numbers.

Two pieces of cannon were fired when we had got about 200 yards from the town-houfe, after which Oftenaco fung the war-fong, in which was a prayer for our fafety thro' the intended journey; this he bellowed out loud enough to be heard at a mile's diftance. We did not march above three miles before we encamped, in order to give time to fome Indians who were to accompany us, but had not yet joined us, which they did in the evening, about fourteen or fifteen in number. Next morning,

morning, the 11th of March, we rofe tolerably early, marching to Little River, about twenty miles from the nation, where we encamped.

At this place had formerly been an Indian town, called Elajoy; and I am furprifed how the natives fhould ever abandon fo beautiful and fertile a fpot. Were it in a more polifhed country, it would make the fineft fituation for a gentleman's feat I ever faw.

We marched the next day to Broad River, which we croffed about four o'clock in the afternoon, without much difficulty, by reafon of the lownefs of the waters; but the river, which is here 700 yards over, runs with great rapidity, and the banks extremely fteep on either fide. We encamped directly, and were all employed in making a large fire to dry ourfelves, as moft of us had got very wet,

Before fun-fet I perceived a confiderable number of Indians paffing at the fame place, whom I at firft imagined to be enemies; but the

arrival

arrival of fome of them fhewed them to be Cherokees, who kept continually dropping in, fo that I was greatly furprifed next morning at their numbers. I demanded where they were going? to which they replied, To Virginia; that the headmen had thought proper to fend a reinforcement, thinking it unfafe for fo fmall a body to march through a country fo much frequented by the enemy, where, if I met with any accident, the blame would fall upon them. I thanked them; but at the fame time told them peremptorily to go back, and give them-felves no further trouble on my account; that I had no occafion for them; and that it would be impoffib e for fo large a body to fub-fift when paffed the hunting grounds, as the people on the frontiers of Virginia had been fo impoverifhed by the late war, they would not be able to fupply us with provifions. This made no impreffion on them, and they marched on without faying another word, and perfifted in going, notwithftanding all the efforts Ofte-co and I could make to prevent them. Indeed I was more earneft to have them return, as I
found

found it was the scent of presents, more than the
desire of escorting me, that was the real motive
of all this good will.

We left the camp the next day, about 165
in number, and marched without any extraordinary occurrence till the 15th, about mid-day,
when we heard our scouts on the left (for we
always kept on both flanks) fire pretty quick
after one another, and in less than a minute
seventeen or eighteen buffaloes ran in amongst
us, before we discovered them, so that several of
us had like to have been run over, especially the
women, who with some difficulty sheltered
themselves behind the trees. Most of the men
fired, but, firing at random, one only was killed,
tho' several more wounded. Our scouts likewise killed another, and brought in the best
parts of the meat, all which was cooked over-
night for our departure next morning.

After passing a very disagreeable night on account of the rain, which, as the evening had been
clear, I had taken no precaution to shelter my-
self

felf againft. We had as difagreeable a march, it proved very rainy, and were again obliged to encamp to a great difadvantage for the convenience of good water.

On the 17th, about two o'clock in the afternoon, we met an Indian who left the Great Ifland fome time after me, with a party of ten or twelve, deftined to Williamfburg, who, after he had eat, drank, and fmoaked, told us the party that he belonged to had been attacked two days before; that two of them had been killed, two or three taken, and the reft difperfed; that he had reafon to believe there were a great many of the enemy upon the path, as he had feen a great many tracks and other figns.

On this intelligence, Oftenaco ordered all his men to frefh prime their guns, and thofe that had bows and arrows to put them in readinefs, fending out fome fcouts, and defiring all to keep a good look-out. After thefe difpofitions we parted with the fugitive Indian, and continued our route. At night our fcouts came in, and informed

formed us, that they had feen fome old tracks, and a piece of an old red waiftcoat, dropped by the enemy, to inform us they were thereabouts. We made large fires to dry ourfelves, while Oftenaco, and four or five others, took out and waved their eagles tails, then turning towards the place where the tracks had been difcovered, gave the war-hoop feveral times extremely loud. This was to let the enemy know, if within hearing, and difpofed for an engagement, where he and his party lay. This however Oftenaco probably would not have done, had he not confided in the number of his party, being greatly fuperior to what commonly go to make war on one another. Before the Indians went to fleep, he gave them a ftrong caution, and inftructions how to act in cafe they were attacked.

We decamped pretty early next morning, in order, if poffible, to reach the Great Ifland that day; but the fcouts had not been out an hour before fome returned with an account of frefh tracks and other figns of the enemy. I really expected a fkirmifh with the northern Indians, as they
might

might probably imagine fome Cherokees would return with me when I left their country; and it was probable the party I had received an account of, and had given fo many checks to the Cherokees fince, were ftill waiting.

As we marched very flow, on account of receiving intelligence from our fcouts, which they brought in every two or three hours, we encamped fhort of the Great Ifland about feven or eight miles.

The next morning we were in no great hurry to decamp, as we intended to go no farther than the Great Ifland that day. By this retardment each man had time to put his arms in proper order. We fet out about eleven o'clock, and, after four or five miles march, Oftenaco defired me to go before, to fee if any of the enemy were there. The northern Indians being at peace with us, was urged as a fufficient protection, tho', at fetting out, they feemed a little apprehenfive of my falling into fuch defperadoes hands, or rather of their lofing their fhare of the

prefents

prefents. I was to tell the enemy, if I met them, that the Cherokees were but few in number, and but indifferently armed; after which Sumpter and I were furnifhed with horfes, and went forward pretty brifkly, till we reached Holfton's River, the croffing place of which was within a mile of Fort Robinfon. We had not forded above half-way over, when we heard the report of a gun, which made us conclude that our fufpicions of the enemy's being there were but too juftly grounded; we rode gently towards the fort to make our obfervations; but no enemy appearing, on entering the clear ground about the fort, and perceiving fome fmoak from one of the chimnies, we rode within an hundred yards of it, and hallowed, but nobody appearing, we went to the gate, and gave another hoop, which, to my great furprife, inftead of the enemy, brought a white man out of one of the houfes, whom I immediately recollected to be M'Lamore the interpreter, that accompanied the difcomfited party of Cherokees, I lately mentioned, to Virginia,

P   and

and he was foon followed by the man who had fired the gun.

I returned to the party, highly fatisfied at my good fortune, in not being obliged to difpleafe the Indians, by breaking thro' fo difagreeable and dangerous a commiffion, who had already croffed the river when I joined them.

We found in the fort eleven or twelve hundred weight of flour, left by the garrifon when they evacuated the place, which abundantly recompenfed the Indians for all their fatigues.

We remained here all next day to reft ourfelves, and mend our mockafons, tho' fuch fine weather was fcarce to be loft, confidering the very bad we had experienced moft of the way from the Cherokee country; this made me extremely anxious to be going forward, but the Indians feldom hurry themfelves when they were to leave fuch good cheer, after having paffed moft of the way without bread. I was informed

formed by M'Lamore, that the flour had been
left for want of horfes to carry it away, as well
as the goods I had obferved in one of the ftore-
houfes, belonging to a private trader ; that the
northern Indians, after defeating the fmall party to which he belonged, and taking him and
two more prifoners, came to the fort, where,
notwithftanding our alliance with them, they
deftroyed a great quantity of the flour and
goods, and carried a great quantity more away,
as well as the man that had the care of them ;
but that, after fome days march, all the prifoners found means to make their efcape : that
they two returned to the fort, one propofing to
wait my coming, and return with me to Virgi
nia, and M'Lamore to go back to the Cherokee
country.

I next day intreated Oftenaco to order his
men to get ready for the march, as the weather
was fine, and it would be agreeable travelling ;
but notwithftanding all he or I could fay, not a
man of them would ftir ; their excufe was, that
one of their horfes was loft, and the owner out

in search of him. We waited his return till night, when he came, but no horse was to be found. I was very much mortified at this accident, as I was anxious to know what was become of my camp-equipage, cloaths, &c. I had left at Fort Attakullakulla.

On the 22d, we rose early in the morning, to make a good day's march, but the horse was not found till near twelve o'clock: I then thought our immediate departure certain, but was again disappointed; the person who had the care of the goods, missing a piece of broadcloth, charged the Indians with the theft, and a general search was made to no purpose. Ostenaco then ordered all within the fort; while he and the conjuror went into the house from whence it was stole, to beg the devil's advice about recovering it. The conjuror might perhaps have saved himself that trouble, for tho' I am at a loss to guess in what manner, I am inclined to believe he had as great a hand in the loss as in the recovery of it. I desired him to trouble himself no farther about it, chusing

ing

ing rather to pay for it, than be detained any longer; but all I could fay could not divert him, from his conjuring, which however furnifhed me with a few more of their oddities.

After ftaying fome time, the conjuror fallied out blindfolded, and groped about, till he came to the fkirts of the woods, where, pulling off the blind, he went ftraight forwards, a confiderable way, and returned in about five minutes with the broad-cloth on his fhoulders. I obferved his cheek tied up with a bit of twine, which, when untied, bled very much. I gave the conjuror two yards as a reward for playing the fool, and we marched forward, encamping about ten miles from the fort.

We called in our way at Fort Attakullakulla, which was likewife evacuated, looked for my cloaths, &c. but they were all ftolen and carried off by the foldiers, except a fmall trunk, with a few trifles, I found afterwards at New River.

Some

Some time after, we met Capt. Ifrael Chrif-
tian going with a cargo of goods, to trade
in the Cherokee country. I here endeavoured
fo fend back the greateft part of the Indians;
but notwithftanding all the perfuafions the
Captain and I could make ufe of, not a man of
them would return, till the Captain promifed
the fame prefents to thofe that would go back,
as would be given to thofe that went forward,
not doubting but that he would be reimburfed,
as the charge of victualling of them would be
entirely faved; but as this expence fell entirely
upon me, as will appear in the fequel, it was
rather taking the burthen off me than off the
public. I am heartily forry, however, this gentleman has fuffered, as well as myfelf, for his
good intentions, and more fo, that it is not in my
power to difcharge the public debt, and reimburfe him. But even by this we could only re-
duce our number to about feventy-two.

We called at Fort Lewis, where we found
William Shorey the interpreter, who, by order
of Col. Stephen, had waited our coming, to accompany

company the Indians to Williamſburg. I received here between ſeventy and eighty pounds
that was due to me, which came very oppor-
tunely to defray our expences to Williamſburg;
where we arrived in about eleven days after our
departure from Fort Lewis.

On my arrival, I waited on the Governor,
who ſeemed ſomewhat diſpleaſed with the
number of Indians that had forced themſelves
upon me Orders however were iſſued out
for their accommodation, and a few days after a
council was called, at which Oſtenaco, and ſome
of the principal Indians, attended After the
uſual ceremonies, and mutual promiſes of
friendſhip, the Indians were diſmiſſed, and pre
ſents ordered them, to the amount of 125 *l.* cur-
rency; 12 *l.* 10 *s.* for Oſtenaco, the ſame ſum
to be ſent back to King Kanagatucko, and the
reſt to be divided among the party, who ſeemed
much diſpleaſed when it came to be divided,
being, as they ſaid, like nothing among them.
I was apprehenſive of ſome bad conſequence
ſhould they return diſſatisfied, and therefore advanced

vanced pretty confiderably out of my own pocket to content them.

A few days before they were to depart for their own country, Mr. Horrocks invited Oftenaco and myfelf to fup with him at the College, where, amongft other curiofities, he fhewed him the picture of his prefent Majefty. The chief viewed it a long time with particular attention; then turning to me, " Long," faid he, " have I wifhed to fee the king my father; " this is his refemblance, but I am determined " to fee himfelf; I am now near the fea, and " never will depart from it till I have obtained " my defires." He afked the Governor next day, who, tho' he at firft refufed, on Oftenaco's infifting fo ftrongly upon it, gave his confent. He then defired, as I had been with him fo long, that I might accompany him to England: this I was to do at my own expence; but the Governor told me he would recommend me to the minifter of ftate, which he did in as ftrong terms as I could defire.

I was

I was then upon the point of entering into a very advantageous commerce, which I quitted to pleafe the Indians, and preferve them ours, yet wavering to the French intereft. I prepared every thing neceffary for my voyage; but this was not my only expence, the Indians having no money, expect the perfon who travels with them to treat them with whatever they take a fancy to.

We fet out for Hampton about the begining of May, where we were to embark; but contrary winds, and other delays, retarded us till the 15th, during which time it generally coft me between 15 and 20 s. per day.

We had very fine weather during the whole voyage, yet both the Indians and myfelf were fea-fick all the way. We parted with a convoy we had under our care off Newfoundland, in a very thick fog, notwithftanding all the efforts Capt. Blake could make, by ringing bells, and firing every quarter of an hour, to keep them together, tho' I afterwards heard him fe-

Q   verely

verely accufed in England of taking this opportunity to leave his charge.

We had the misfortune here to lofe the interpreter Shorey, who was much regretted by us all, but efpecially by the Indians, as he was a thorough mafter of their language. He had lingered fome time in a confumption, caught in paffing a fmall river, for, being drunk, his Indian fpoufe plunged him in to fober him, but was unable to draw him out, and had not fome Indians come to her affiftance he muft have been drowned This was an effectual means of fobering him, but by it he contracted the malady that carried him off.

During our voyage the Indians conceived very advantageous ideas of our naval force; the Captain having chafed and brought too about fixteen fail, found them all to be Englifh or neutral veffels, on which the Cherokees concluded the French and Spaniards were certainly afraid to put to fea.

On

On the 16th of June we arrived at Plymouth, where, before we went on fhore, the Indians had their defire of feeing a large man of war gratified, by being carried on board the Revenge, a feventy-four gun fhip, with which they were equally pleafed and furprifed.

While in the boat that took us to fhore, Oftenaco, painted in a very frightful manner, fung a folemn dirge with a very loud voice, to return God thanks for his fafe arrival. The loudnefs and uncouthnefs of his finging, and the oddity of his perfon, drew a vaft crowd of boats, filled with fpectators, from all the fhips in the harbour; and the landing-place was fo thronged, that it was almoft impoffible to get to the inn, where we took poft for London.

We ftopped at Exeter, where the Indians were fhewed the cathedral, but, contrary to my expectation, were as little ftruck as if they had been natives of the place. They were much better pleafed the next day with Lord Pembroke's feat at Wilton, till they faw the ftatue

of

of Hercules with his club uplifted, which they thought fo dreadful that they begged immediately to be gone.

We arrived the next day in London, without any other accident than the breaking down of the chaife in which the Indians were, but happily none of them were hurt.

Capt. Blake waited on Lord Egremont, to acquaint him with our arrival. We were immediately fent for, and, after fome few queftions, difmiffed. Lodgings were ordered, and taken by Mr. N—— Caccanthropos. We were again fent for by Lord Egremont, but more to gratify the curiofity of fome of his friends than about bufinefs. I however took this opportunity of flipping my letter of recommendation into his Lordfhip's hands, which he read, and affured me he would fhew it to the King that day; telling me to let the Indians or myfelf want for nothing; that as I was a perfect ftranger, he had ordered Mr. Caccanthropos to provide whatever we defired

As

My firft care was to equip the Indians. I attended Mr. Caccanthropos, to order all after the mode of their own country.

As feveral days paffed before I had any further orders, the Indians became extremely anxious to fee the King. " What is the reafon," faid they, " that we are not admitted to fee the " Great King our Father, after coming fo far for " that purpofe?" I was obliged to reply, " That " his Majefty was indifpofed, and could not " be waited on till perfectly recovered," which in fome meafure pacified them. We were taken not long after to court; but I was only afked a few queftions, of which I gave the interpretation to the Indians that might be moft favourably received.

The uncommon appearance of the Cherokees began to draw after them great crowds of people of all ranks; at which they were fo much difpleafed, that home became irkfome to them, and they were forever teizing me to take them to fome public diverfion. Their favourite

rite was Sadler's-Wells; the activity of the performers, and the machinery of the panto-mime, agreeing beſt with their notions of di-verſion. They were likewiſe very fond of Ra-nelagh, which, from its form, they compared to their town-houſe; but they were better pleaſ-ed with Vauxhall, tho' it was always againſt my inclination I accompanied them there, on ac-count of the ungovernable curioſity of the peo-ple, who often intruded on them, and induced them to drink more than ſufficient. Once, in particular, one of the young Indians got ex-tremely intoxicated, and committed ſeveral ir-regularities, that ought rather to be attributed to thoſe that enticed them, than to the ſimple Indians, who drank only to pleaſe them. I cannot indeed cite ſobriety as their characteriſ-tic; but this I can ſay, theſe exceſſes never happened at home. A bottle of wine, a bowl of punch, and a little cyder, being the ordina-ry conſumption of the three Indians, Sumpter, and myſelf; and as we were ſeldom at home, it could not put the nation to a great expence. If the bills given in for theſe articles were to

the

the greateſt degree exceſſive, let them that charged them anſwer who conſumed them; I only know that no more was ever drank by us.

This was not the only thing laid to my charge; I was accuſed of receiving money for admiſſion to ſee the Indians. The ſheep was accuſed by the wolf of rapine, who carried his point. He was a thorough-paced under-courtier; the ſheep, a raw Virginian, who, ignorant of little arts, innocently believed others as ho- 'neſt as himſelf, and could never believe ſuch impudence exiſted, as to accuſe another of crimes his conſcience aſſured him he was ſole actor of. I was ſo prepoſſeſſed with theſe o- pinions, that I can ſcarce as yet, however ſe- verely I have felt it, believe that ſome men have no ideas of conſcience, and eſteem it the prejudices of education, and a narrow mind; and that blaſting an innocent perſon's character, whenever it anſwered their ends, or that rob- bing the nation was no crime, when they could eſcape puniſhment.

It

It was a long time before I knew any thing of thefe money-taking works. The following accident was what brought it to light. Finding myfelf entirely confined by the continual crowds of vifitors, I refolved to leffen the number, by ordering the fervants to admit none but people of fafhion. This was what would have been at once agreeable to the Indians, and raifed their ideas of the Englifh nation. So far from thefe orders being complied with, the whole rabble of the town was ufhered in the next day. Not a little mortified, I complained to Lord Egremont, who, already perhaps prepoffeffed againft me, only told me coldly, that he would fpeak of it to Mr. Caccanthropos. At my return, tho' I found the houfe full of people, I faid nothing more.

Some days after, Sumpter, who had contracted fome genteel acquaintance, fome of whom he was bringing to fee the Indians, was ftopped by the fervant, Mr. Caccanthropos's relation, who refufed to admit them without money. The young man, who had faced all dangers for the

fervice

ſervice of his country in the war, who had been ſo highly inſtrumental in ſaving us from the dangers that threatened us in going to their country, and had accompanied us ever ſince, received that affront from an inſolent ſervant; but not being able to bear the inſult, he took a warrior's ſatisfaction, and knocked him down. A blunt Virginian ſoldier cannot know the laws of England, as little can he bear an inſult from ſo mean a quarter.

The ſervant informed his kinſman, who came next day open-mouthed, threatening Sumpter with the crown-office. He next gave me ſuch ſcurrilous language, that I was perfectly at a loſs how to retort it adequately; I had ſubject enough, but being accuſtomed to gentlemen's company, I could ſcarce underſtand his dialect: piqued, however, at the ſtinging truths I told him, he threatened me with confinement alſo, aſſaying to intimidate me from publiſhing them, by reminding me that he was a juſtice of the peace. Happily I reflected on the diſparity of his years and ſtrength to mine; my hands had

R

near

near difgraced me, by ftriking a perfon I fo much every way defpifed. He dared not, however, put his threats into execution; his only vengeance for affronting me, was ordering the people of the houfe to feed us for the future on ox-cheek, cow-heel, and fuch like dainties, fit entertainment for Indians accuftomed to only the choiceft parts of the beaft, and very fit to raife their opinion of England. I however underftanding Lord Egremont's orders in a different light, took care to provide whatever was requifite for the Indians, avoiding at the fame time all appearance of extravagance.

Sumpter's company were not the only perfons to whom admittance was refufed; the fame fervant had even the impudence to ftop Lady T-r—l-y. Her Ladyfhip fent immediately for Mrs. Quin, the gentlewoman of the houfe, to enquire if I encouraged the fervants in taking money for feeing the Indians. Mrs. Quin fet her Ladyfhip to rights in that particular; but ftill whatever exactions thefe fellows made, the public generally laid to me. I was cleared, however,

ever, by Cacanthropos himself, who once at-
tempted to ftop Mr. Montague; and his fear and
confufion on finding whom he had offended,
in fome meafure revenged me.

Soon after thefe difturbances, orders were
given by Lord Egremont, that no perfon whatever fhould be admitted, without an order from
himfelf, or Mr. Wood, under Secretary of State:
but inftead of the throngs decreafing by this
order, it rather increafed; and I really believe
few perfons have more friends than Mr. Wood,
if he knew but half of thofe that were ufhered
in under that name; nay, grown bolder by that
fanction, they preffed into the Indians dreffing
room, which gave them the higheft difguft, thefe
people having a particular averfion to being
ftared at while dreffing or eating; on which laft
occafion, if I was irkfome myfelf, judge what a
crowd of ftrangers muft be. They were fo dif-
gufted, that they grew extremely fhy of being
feen, fo that I had the greateft difficulty in pro-
curing Lord C—t—f—d a fight of them; on
which, being a little angry, I was afterwards in-

R 2   formed,

formed his Lordfhip had been offended at fomething I am yet a ftranger to. It ever was againft my inclination to give offence to even the loweft clafs of mankind, much lefs to Lord C—t—f—d.

I was not only, however, accufed of receiving money at our lodgings, but at the public places we frequented. To this I anfwer, fo far from making by them, it generally coft me pretty confiderable to the fervants, befides coach-hire; for tho' one was allowed us, we could command it no oftener than Mr. Cacanthropos was pleafed to do us that favour; and this expence was entirely out of my own pocket, without any profpect of reimburfement.

As to the charge laid againft me, the proprietors are ftill alive, and any perfon that entertains the fmalleft doubt, may, and would oblige me, by enquiring of themfelves, whether I ever demanded or took directly or indirectly any money or confideration whatever from them.

But

But let us now return to the Indians. Some time before they left England, they were admitted to a conference with his Majesty at St. James's. Oftenaco's speech on that occasion contained nothing more than protestations of friendship, faithful alliance, &c. To which an answer was afterwards given in writing, to be interpreted in their own country, as I was not conversant enough in their language to translate it; though I understood whatever they said, especially the speech, which I gave word for word to his Majesty, as Shorey had likewise explained it before his death, except the last part, which was so much in my favour that I was obliged to suppress it, and was in some confusion in finding wherewith to supply it; till I at last told his Majesty, that it was only in some manner a repetition of the first part of his discourse.

They were struck with the youth, person, and grandeur of his Majesty, and conceived as great an opinion of his affability as of his power, the greatness of which may be seen

on

on my telling them in what manner to behave; for finding Oftenaco preparing his pipe
to fmoak with his Majefty, according to the
Indian cuftom of declaring friendfhip, I told
him he muft neither offer to fhake hands or
fmoak with the King, as it was an honour for
the greateft of our nation to kifs his hand.
You are in the right, fays he, for he com-
mands over all next to the Man above, and
no-body is his equal. Their ideas were likewife greatly increafed by the number of fhips
in the river, and the warren at Woolwich,
which I did not fail to fet out to the greateft
advantage, intimating that our Sovereign had
many fuch ports and arfenals round the king-
dom.

Some days before the Indians fet out on
their return to their own country, Lord Egremont fent for me, and informed me that the
Indians were to be landed at Charles Town;
but this was fo contrary to their inclination,
that Oftenaco pofitively declared, that, unlefs
he was to land in Virginia, he would not ftir

a ftep

a ftep from London. His Lordfhip then defired me to tell them that they fhould land at
Virginia, but at the fame time gave me to
underftand, that the fhip being to be ftationed
at Charles Town, they muft abfolutely be
landed there. I informed his Lordfhip that
it was entirely out of my power to accompany
them there, having fcarce five fhillings remaining out of the 130 pounds I had received,
the heft part of which I laid out for the Indians ufe, rather than apply to Mr. Cacanthropos;
that I was ready to obey his Lordfhip, if he
would pleafe to order me wherewith to defray
my expences from Charles Town to Virginia.
My Lord replied, that no more could be advanced; that if I refufed to accompany them,
others muft be found that would.

Sumpter was immediately fent for by Mr.
Wood; but he refufed the employ till he had
obtained my approbation; nay, I was obliged
to ufe the moft perfuafive arguments to deter-
mine him to go; fo that it was then in my
power (had I been the man I was reprefented)
to have made what terms I pleafed, fince the
Indians

Indians would not have gone without one of us, and Sumpter had too much honour to accompany them to my prejudice. I fcorned fo low an action; but told Sumpter, that tho' I had only afked my expences, which might amount to about twenty or twenty-five pounds, there was a difference between his going and mine; that he muft make the voyage in the view of advantage, whereas I had fought none in it, except returning to my native country. The terms agreed on were fifty pounds in hand, and a hundred on his arrival; and it was even in his power to infift on more.

Had I really had the money, I fhould not have troubled the government, or deferted the Indians; but to be landed in a ftrange country without money, and far from my friends, did not feem very eligible. I was extremely rejoiced at the young man's advantage; yet could not but think it hard to be left in England for fo fmall, fo reafonable a demand, as no other bufinefs than the Indian affairs had brought me there, when feven times the fum

was

was granted to another. Lord Egremont indeed had informed me that the King, in confideration of my fervices in the Cherokee country, had ordered me a Lieutenancy in an old regiment, which I fhould receive from Sir Jeffery Amherft in North America, and pofitively affured me, I fhould never be reduced to half-pay; fo that, had I been in my own country, I had reafon to be fatisfied; but I had no money to carry me there.

The Indians foon re-imbarked in the fame veffel that brought them, and left England about the 25th of Auguft; fo that I was now entirely at my own expence, without money or friends. I continually folicited Lord Egremont for money fufficient to defray my paffage to Virginia, during which my circumftances were continually growing worfe. I difclofed my diftreffed fituation to a Gentleman with whom I had contracted an intimacy, who advifed me to prefent a petition to the King, affuring me at the fame time, that he would fpeak to a Nobleman of his acquaintance to

S   fecond

fecond it. I went to the Park next morning with a petition that my friend approved, but was very irrefolute whether to deliver it or not; my neceffities, however, at laft determined me.

Some days after I was fent for by Mr. Wood, who, after a fhort reverie, told me, that Lord Egremont had ordered a hundred pounds, *if that would do.* I knew from whence thefe orders came; but, as he induftrioufly avoided mentioning the petition, I only anfwered that it would. I was fince informed, that two hundred pounds were ordered me; but even one had been fufficient, had I received it at one payment; but getting it at different times, before I had paid my debts, and received it all, I was again run fhort.

Upon applying to the treafury for this money, I was afked by Mr. M--t-n if I was not the perfon that accompanied the Cherokees to England? On anfwering in the affirmative, he

desired

defired me to revife Mr. Cacanthropos's accounts, exclaiming againft their extravagance. On looking over them, I did not find them quite fo extravagant as I expected, being only overcharged by about 150 pounds; but what I mean by overcharging, is what the Indians never had ; for I cannot be fo fenfible of what was overcharged by other means. *The Indians being remarkable for their fkill in mathematics, but unfortunate in not having fufficient workmen among them, he had wifely ftocked the whole nation with inftruments.* Mr. W——— the optician's bill being to the amount, as near as I can remember, of fifty odd pounds in thefe coftly play-things for the Cherokees; but as neither they nor I had ever feen or heard of fuch inftruments, although I was defired to order all things they might have occafion for, as beft judge of what was neceffary, I am inclined to think they were turned to a much better purpofe. There was another bill from Mr. L——d for ftocks and ftockings, to the amount of forty odd pounds. Wampum, I fuppofe, is become fo fcarce among the In-

S 2

dians,

dians, that they are refolved to adopt the Englifh cuftom of ftocks. It is a little unconfcion-
able to have forty pounds worth in change;
but then Mr. Cacanthropos can eafily account
for that. Thefe people wear a great deal of
vermilion, and are naturally not over cleanly, fo
of confequence their ftocks would very foon be
dirty; befides, they cannot be expected to
wear fo long as everlafting wampum. Very
true! very provident, Sir! And I fuppofe you
prefume too the bufhes would tear a great
many ftockings; but if I can judge of Indians, they are a great deal wifer than to be fine
in ftockings among the briars, at the expence
of their legs, which good leggons keep un-
fcratched, and a great deal warmer. This
does not however, dear Sir, prevent my admir
ing your provident views; they are abfolutely
too ftriking ever to admit of that.

Five yards of fuperfine dove-coloured cloth,
at a guinea a yard, was charged at the woollen-
draper's. Ah! dear Sir, you were fhort fighted
here; two yards and three-quarters make a
match-

match-coat and leggons, five yards will not make two; a coarser cloth would have suited Indians, and another colour would have pleafed them much better; for I am much miftaken if thefe are not the only Indians that ever wore other than their favourite colours of red and blue; but the laceman's bill will clear up this affair. Let me fee! Vellum lace, broad and narrow: Was it for button holes for a Cherokee mantle? Sure Oftenaco never once had the ridiculous fancy of putting ufelefs, and folely ornamental, buttons upon a match-coat; where the duce then were the button-holes placed? But I may, I believe, give a hiftory of that affair, without being mafter of an uncommon penetration. A certain *Man-Killer* wanting a holiday fuit to appear in, at the inftallation of fome royal and noble knights of the garter — but here fome critic, a pretended judge of Indian affairs, will perhaps fay, that Indians have no fuch inftallations, and that they would never become the laughing-ftock of their countrymen, by being fwathed up in Englifh cloaths. Well, fharp-eyed critic, good cloaths will never want
wearers;

wearers; it is a pity good things fhould be loft, and the gentleman that provided them muft abfolutely be obliged to wear them himfelf, fince the Indians will not. What goodnefs! Condefcend to wear the Indians refufals! *O tempora! O mores!* The wafherwoman's bill, with many others, I had already paid; but as it had not paid toll *en paffant*, it found its way into the treafury, with an encreafe of five or fix pounds, being juft as much again as the contents of the bill; fo fumming up the gentleman's profits on what was really received, I imagined it to be about *cent. per cent.*

Mr. Martin defired me to take the accounts home to revife at my leifure, which I foon after returned with alterations, little to the honour of the original accomptant, however great his fkill in figures. But as his character has been fufficiently known in feveral late affairs, I fhall fpend no more of my time, or the reader's patience, in quoting numerable inftances of the fame dye. I fhall only mention the injury done to Mr. Quin, whofe houfe was fo fpoiled

by

by the rabble that came to fee the Indians, that he was at a great expence to put it to rights; but inftead of Mr. Cacanthropos's allowing out of the immenfe profits of the fhow, wherewith to repair the damage, he got him to fign a receipt in full, and then curtailed and perquifited three pounds.

But it is now time to return to my own misfortunes. After paying the debts I had contracted, my finances were, as I have already hinted, fo low, that I had not wherewith to defray my paffage. I made no doubt of getting credit for a part till my arrival. At the Virginia Coffee-houfe I found a Captain of my acquaintance, bound to Virginia, into whofe hands I depofited ten guineas to fecure my paffage; but the fhip, thro' fome unaccountable delays, did not quit her moorings till December, when the Captain told me fhe would go round to Portfmouth, which place he thought would be more convenient for me to embark at. I readily acquiefced with this, as I thought my paffage would be long enough without any addition.

dition. But before I arrived at Portſmouth, my money ran ſo ſhort, that I was forced to borrow of the landlord, to pay the laſt ſtage. I had ſlaid here nine or ten days, in expectation of the ſhip, when a letter arrived from the Captain, to deſire me to return im_mediately to London, or repair to Deal, as his employers had ſent him orders not to touch at Portſmouth, but to proceed immediately to ſea. I was thunderſtruck. The tavern-keeper had juſt ſent in his bill for payment, the inſtant I received this letter. I was obliged to depoſit cloaths and other effects to the amount of forty pounds, and borrow ten guineas to return.

As ſoon as I arrived at London, I ſent my ſervant to enquire if the ſhip had fallen down the river, who ſhortly after returned with infor-mation that ſhe had. I then went to Graveſ-end, where my money running ſhort again, I had recourſe to the landlady. I ſent to the of-fice, to know if ſuch a ſhip had cleared, and was agreeably informed there had not. After expecting the ſhip four or five days, I ſent my

ſervant

fervant to London, to procure fome money
on my watch, with orders to inquire after
the fhip at every place between London and
Gravefend. On his return the next day he informed me the fhip, with feveral more, were
frozen up at Deptford. I now began to be
under the greateft uneafinefs about my return
to Virginia, fate feeming determined to detain
me where misfortunes daily increafed. I fent
to the Captain for the ten guineas I had advanced for my paffage, fince I found it impoffible to go with him, and returned to London,
where my firft concern was, to enquire at the
war-office whether there had lately arrived
any returns from Sir Jeffery Amherft? I was
informed there had, and, on turning over the
books, found myfelf appointed Lieutenant in
the forty-fecond or Royal Highland regiment
of foot, with feveral months fubfiftence due
to me, which I received foon after from Mr.
Drummond, the agent, to whom I made
known my circumftances, intreating him to
lend me fifty pounds more, without which I
found it impoffible to get out of England. He

T   obligingly

obligingly told me, that if I could get any gentleman to accept a bill payable in four months, he would willingly advance that fum. I applied to a gentleman in the city, who was kind enough to accept the bill.

I agreed with a Captain of a fhip bound to Virginia, about the middle of March, and paid him thirty-two guineas for my wife's paffage and my own; for I had married, or rather made a young lady a companion of my misfortunes fome time before; but her father having refufed his confent to our union, had the barbarity to deny us the leaft affiftance, nay, refufed me even ten guineas that I found deficient, after paying my debts, and laying in what was neceffary. All affairs being feemingly fettled, I went to Billingfgate overnight to fave expences, by going in a Gravefend boat the next day, but was prevented by a bailiff, who, as foon as I was up, arrefted me, at the fuit of a perfon, who, not making any demand upon me, in my confufion I forgot, or rather did not know where to find.

I was

I was carried immediately to Wood-Street Compter, where I wrote to a friend for money to difcharge it but being ; difappointed, I was obliged to pay away the little I had referved for my expences, fo that I had but two fhillings left. We now embarked for Gravefend ; but before we had got two miles down the river, the boat ran foul of a fhip's hawfer, by which we were almoft overfet. We ftaid a confiderable time, to no purpofe, to get her clear, but were obliged at laft to go afhore and return to Billingfgate, where we ftaid all night, and next morning, for want of money to difcharge our reckoning, I was forced to fell a gold feal that coft me four guineas, for only eleven fhillings. `

I then embarked in another boat, and got within four miles of Gravefend without any further interruption ; but the tide being fpent here, we were obliged to walk to Gravefend on foot, where the fhip came down, and anchored next morning.

The

The Captain informed me, that two gentlemen and a lady, paffengers in the fhip, would be glad that we fhould all dine together. This I readily confented to, but begged a couple of guineas that I had been deficient in my old reckoning at the White-Hart. Unwilling to borrow any more from the Captain, I fent my fervant with a pair of new crimfon velvet breeches that coft me three guineas, who returned with thirteen fhillings that he had raifed on them. Being now on board, I thought myfelf fecure from all further demands or impediments; but we no fooner arrived in the Downs than my fervant left me, and demanded four guineas for the time he had ferved me; a gentleman that was going a-fhore did me the favour to pay him the money he demanded.

This detail may feem very dry to a reader; but this muft effectually convince the public, that had I made money of the Indians, nay, partook of the great fums that were clandeftinely made by them, I fhould not have been

fo foon reduced to the neceffities I under-
went.

After fome difficulties in getting out, we
had a very good paffage to Virginia. I ftaid
there but juft long enough to fettle my affairs,
and then fet out for New York to wait on Sir
Jeffery Amherft for my commiffion; but to
fave the expences of going by land, I embarked in an old worm-eaten floop that be
longed to a gentleman at New York, who had
been obliged to fend a Captain to bring her
home, her former one having deferted her in
that ruinous condition. She had, however,
tolerable pumps and fails, and three good
hands befides the Captain.

The firft day the wind was very fair, and
gave us hopes it would continue fo the whole
paffage, but fhifting next day to the north-
weft quarter, we experienced a perfect hurri-
cane, in which the veffel made water fo faft,
that the men were conftantly at the pumps to
clear her. The fea ran fo high, and the veffel

was

was ſo old and crazy, that I expected each
wave would daſh her to pieces; the third day
we ſhewed a little ſail, though it continued
blowing very freſh till evening, when it became pretty fair; yet ſhe ſtill made water at a
prodigious rate, and extremely fatigued the
men. We ſaw land next day, but were be-
calmed till the morning after, when a freſh
gale ſpringing up fair, we went at the rate of
eight knots an hour till four in the afternoon,
when a pilot came on board; the Captain told
him that he muſt run the veſſel quite to New
York that night, as he had no cable to bring
her to an anchor. Had I known this circum-
ſtance before, which even the pilot was aſto-
niſhed at, I ſhould not, I believe, have truſted
ſo much to fair weather. We arrived, however, ſafe at New York.

I waited next morning on Sir Jeffery Am-
herſt, who gave me my commiſſion, with orders immediately to join my regiment, which
was then on its way to Pittſburg. I dined
with his Excellency next day; after which he
told

told me to wait on Col. Reid, and not be in a hurry to join my regiment. A packet it feems had arrived from England the fame day I received my commiffion, which, I fuppofe, brought a lift of the officers to be reduced on half pay, and on waiting on Col. Reid, I found I was of the number   I related Lord Egremont's affurances to the contrary, and produced this his Lordfhip's Letter to Sir Jeffery Amherft in my favour.

" Sir,   *Whitehall, July* 23, 1762.

" Mr. Fauquier, Lieutenant Governor of Virginia, having reprefented the long and very ufeful fervices, particulaily in the Cherokee country, of Mr. Timberlake, and having ftrongly recommended him to fome mark of his Majefty's royal favour, and Mr. Timberlake having accompanied fome chiefs of the Cherokee nation to London, where he has conftantly attended them, and has conducted himfelf entirely to the King's fatisfaction: I am to acquaint you that his Majefty, in confideration

deration of the above fervices of Mr. Timberlake, has been pleafed to command me to fignify
to you his royal pleafure, that you fhould appoint
him to the firft Lieutenancy in an old regiment,
which fhall become vacant in North America,
after you receive this letter.   I am, &c.

(Signed)

EGREMONT.

The Colonel, on perufing it, was of the fame
opinion, that certainly his Lordfhip never intended me to be reduced.   I went again to wait
on the General; but being denied admiffion, I
immediately inquired for a veffel bound to Virginia, and having at laft found one, returned
home after fpending between twenty and thirty
guineas to no purpofe; for had it been his
Lordfhip's intention to have had me reduced, I
could have been no more in a young regiment,
without fending me to New York, in North
America, for a commiffion.

I re-

I remained at home till January 1764, when the General Affembly of the colony met for the difpatch of public bufinefs, whither I repaired to petition for my expences from the Cherokee country to Williamfburg; which, however, were greatly fuperior to the accounts I gave in, left they fhould judge any of them unreafonable. While my money lafted the Indians wanted for nothing, and I am ftill confiderably indebted on their account.

I gained a majority, and a committee was appointed to look into my accounts, who told me it was to be paid by the council, out of the money for contingent charges, and not by the colony. After waiting a confiderable time, at a very great expence, whilft urgent bufinefs required my prefence elfewhere, I at laft got the favour of Mr. Walthoe, Clerk of the Council, to undertake prefenting my petition and accounts to the Governor and Council, in my abfence, which he did at the next meeting, and foon after fent me the following letter.

U   " Sir,

"Sir,   *Williamsburg, Feb.* 3, 1764.

" It would have afforded me a very sensible pleasure, had I been enabled by the resolution of the Council to have returned a satisfactory answer to your letter of the 26th of last month. In compliance with your request, I the last day of the sessions presented to the board your account, and the opinion of the committee to which it was referred. It was maturely considered and debated, and, extremely contrary to my hopes, disapproved of and rejected; for this reason principally, that you went, as they were persuaded, not by any order, to the Cherokee nation, but in pursuit of your own profit, or pleasure, * * * * * * * * *, &c.

(Signed)

N. Walthoe."

I was quite astonished to find, on the receipt of this letter, that these gentlemen imagined I had made a party of pleasure to a savage country, in the winter season; or that I went in the view of profit, with a stock of twenty pounds worth
of

of goods, moſt of which I diſtributed amongſt the neceſſitous priſoners. Had I intended profit, I ſhould certainly have taken the ſafeſt way, and a ſufficient quantity of goods to have recompenced me for all my fatigues and danger, as I ſurely did not expect preſents in the Cherokee country.

I went to convince the Indians of our ſincerity, to know the navigation, and to ſerve my country. Let others take care how they precipitate themſelves to ſerve ſo ungrateful a ————. But the reader, by this time, is too well acquainted with the particulars of my journey, to paſs judgment with theſe gentlemen. I have already ſhewn, that my expences and loſſes, during that unfortunate jaunt, was upwards of an hundred pounds in ready money, beſides what I gave them in preſents at their return to their own country, and what I am ſtill indebted for on their account.

It was objected, that I was not ordered. I own it. Do they know Col. Stephen? Did he ever order any officer on ſuch a ſervice? Is my

ſervice

fervice of lefs merit, becaufe I offered myfelf to do what, tho' neceffary, he could not well command? Does the brave volunteer, who defires to mount the breach, merit lefs than the coward, whofe officer compells him to it? No, certainly. We fhould praife and countenance fuch forwardnefs; yet for this fame reafon have I been refufed my expences. Can any one think Col. Stephen would command any officer amongft a favage and unfettled enemy, whofe hands were ftill reeking, as I may fay, with the blood of Demeré and the garrifon of Fort Loudoun, maffacred after they had capitulated, and were marching home according to agreement, who have no laws, and are both judges and executors of their revenge?

I had no written orders. I never doubted they would be called in queftion, tho' verbal. But here are fome extracts of two of Col. Stephen's letters to me, while in the Cherokee country, that may clear up this particular. In one dated Fort Lewis, January 30, 1762, he fays, "Give my compliments to your beft friends,

" and

" and I fhould have been extremely glad to
" have heard that Judd's Friend (i. e. Oftenaco)
" had received the fmall prefent I fent him from
" the Great Ifland. I know no reafon which
" will prevent you and Judd's Friend taking
" your own time to come in, and fhould be glad
" to fee you, &c."

In another, dated Fort Lewis, February 14,
1762, he fays, " The Governor is extremely
" pleafed with Judd's Friend's favours to you,
" and the kindnefs of all the Cherokees, and I
" think it is the better how foon the chiefs
" come in with you."

I was to bring fome chiefs in then: this has
likewife been difputed?

But if I had no written orders, thofe given to
Shorey will prove my verbal ones. The original, among my other papers, is in Mr. Walthoe's hands; but the fubftance, as near as I
can recollect, was as follows: " William Sho-
" rey, you are to wait at Fort Lewis for the
" coming

" coming of Mr. Timberlake, and accompany
" Judd's Friend in quality of interpreter to
Williamſburg. I can rely more upon you
" than on M'Cormack. Pray put the country
" to as little expence as poſſible."

Through theſe continual ſeries of ill fortunes,
I got ſo much in debt, that I was obliged to ſell
my paternal eſtate and negroes. My friends
adviſed me to return to London, promiſing to
ſend me their tobacco, and I to make returns
in ſuch goods as would beſt ſuit the country,
of which I was a tolerable judge. I commu-
nicated this project to many of my acquain-
tances, who gave me great encouragement, and
promiſes of aſſiſtance. Mr. Trueheart, a gentleman of Hanover county, ſo much approved
it, that he propoſed himſelf a partner in the un-
dertaking, as a voyage to England might be the
means of recovering his health, then much on the
decline. I did not heſitate to accept the propoſals
of a perſon of fortune, who could advance money
to carry it into execution. We accordingly begun
our preparations for the voyage, which were already

ready in fome degree of readinefs, when walking one day in Mr. Trueheart's fields, I perceived five Indians coming towards the houfe, in company with one of Mr. Trueheart's fons, whom, upon a nearer view, I recollected to be fome of my Cherokee acquaintance. I enquired of Mr. Trueheart where he found them? He told me at Warwick, enquiring for me, and overjoyed when he offered to conduct them to his father's houfe, where I was, fince they had feared being obliged to go a great way to feek me.

After eating and fmoaking, according to cuf-tom, the headman told me he had orders to find me out, even fhould I be as far off as New-York, to accompany them to Williamfburg, being fent with a talk to the Governor, about bufinefs of the greateft confequence, and the headman hoped I was too much their friend to refufe them that favour. I replied, that the behaviour of the Cherokees to me, while in their country, obliged me to return what lay in my power while they were in mine; that I would never refuse any thing that could be of any advantage to them, but do every thing to ferve them. After refting a couple of days, we fet out, and in two more arrived at Williamfburg. They waited next morning on the Governor to difclofe their bufinefs, which the headman afterwards told me, was to demand a paffage to England, as encroachments were daily made upon them, notwithftanding the proclamation iffued by the King to the contrary; that their hunting grounds, their only fupport, would be foon entirely ruined by the Englifh; that frequent complaints had been made to the Governors to no purpofe, they therefore refolved to feek redrefs in England. Next day a council met on the occafion, and an anfwer promifed the day following. As I had fome particular bufinefs with the Governor, I waited on him the morning the Indians were to have their anfwer. The chief of what the Governor faid concerning them was, that they fhould have applied to Capt. Stuart, at Charles Town, he being fuperintendant for Indian affairs; that if the white people encroached, he faw no way to prevent it, but

but by repelling them by force. I no fooner left the Governor than the Indians came to wait on him. I am unacquainted with what paffed during this interval; but the interpreter came juft after to my lodgings, and told me their demand was refufed; that the headman, who was then down at the Capitol, intended to go to New-York for a paffage; on which I rode down there, to take my leave of them The interpreter then told me, that the headman in-treated me to take them to England, as he un-derftood by Mr. Trueheart's people that I was going over. I replied, that however willing to do the Cherokees any favour, it was utterly out of my power to do that, as their paffage would be a great expence, and my finances ran fo low, I could fcarce defray my own. I fhould then have objected the Governor's orders to the con-trary, if any fuch had ever been given; but I am apt to think they came in a private letter to England many months afterwards. I ftrove to fhuffle the refufal on Mr. Trueheart, hinting that he was a perfon of fortune, and had it in his power; on which they returned back with me, and applied to him.

X

On

On my return, I acquainted Mr. Trueheart with the whole affair, who, moved by their intreaties, and a fenfe of the injuftice done to thefe unfortunate people, who daily fee their poffeffions taken away, yet dare not oppofe it, for fear of engaging in a war with fo puiffant an enemy, contrary to my expectation, agreed to bring them over. One of them died before we fet out, but we proceeded with the other four to York Town. We were already embarked, and weighing anchor, when Mr. Trueheart finding the cabin much lumbered, refolved to take his paffage in another veffel. We were fcarce out of York River, when the wind fhifted directly contrary, and in a little time blew fo hard, that we were obliged to let go another anchor, the veffel having dragged the firft a confiderable way. We got to fea in a day or two after, and proceeded on our voyage to Briftol. The day we made land, one of the Indians, brother to Chucatah the headman, died fuddenly. We faw a fhip lying off Lundy, which we found, on fpeaking with, to be the fame Mr. Trueheart was on board, and that his

fon

son had died on the passage. In a day or two
after our arrival, we set out for London, where
the day after we arrived I went, as Mr. Trueheart knew nothing of the town, to acquaint
Lord H——— of the Indians arrival; but his
Lordship was not at home. I called again
next day, but received the same answer. I went
some time after to the office, and acquainted
one of the Under-Secretaries with their busi-
ness, who told me, as well as I can remember,
that his Lordship would have nothing to do
with them, as they did not come over by au-
thority ; at which Mr. Trueheart and the Indians were greatly displeased : that gentleman,
then, to lessen the expences as much as possible,
took a cheap lodging in Long's-Court, Leices-
ter-Fields, for himself and the Indians, where,
after a short illness, he died on the 6th of November.

This was a great loss to me, and likely to
be severely felt by the Indians, who must have
perished, had I not taken care of them, and
promised payment for their board, &c. I ne-

ver

ver indeed doubted but when Lord H——
fhould be informed with the true fituation of
affairs, he would readily reimburfe me; I fent
him a letter for that purpofe, but received no
anfwer. The Indians began to be very uneafy
at fo long a confinement, as my circumftances
would not permit their going fo often to public diverfions as they fhould have done. They,
therefore, begged to come and live with
me.

I fome time after, the better to accommo-
date them, took a houfe, and gave my note for
their board, which came to £. 29 : 13 : 6.
I wrote again to Lord H——, and received a
verbal anfwer at the office, from Mr.
St—h—e, which was, that his Lordfhip took
very ill my troubling him with thofe letters ·
that fince I had brought the Indians here, I
fhould take them back, or he would take fuch
meafures as I fhould not like. I replied,
fomething haftily, that I had not brought the
Indians, neither would I carry them back:
that his Lordfhip might take what meafures

he

he pleafed ; which I fuppofe offended a cour-
tier accuftomed to more deceitful language.
I am a foldier, and above cringing or bearing
tamely an injury.

But fhould thefe people commence a war,
and fcalp every encroacher, or even others, to
revenge the ill treatment they received while
coming in a peaceable manner to feek redrefs
before they had recourfe to arms, let the
public judge who muft anfwer it ; I muft,
however, lay great part of the blame on Mr.
Cacoanthropos, who, poffeffing the ear of Lord
H———, made fuch an unfavourable report of
me, that either his Lordfhip believed, or pretended to believe them impoftors, or Indians
brought over for a fhew. They were known
by feveral gentlemen in London to be of
power in their own country ; and had not the
government been convinced of that, I fcarce
think they would have fent them home at all.
As to his other fufpicion, even when I had
been fo great a lofer, without hopes of redrefs,
I might have juftified making a fhew of them ;
but

but they were quite private; few knew there were fuch people in London. Nay, I did not enough difabufe the public when that impoftor, who had taken the name of Chucatah, was detected; fo the public, without further examination, imagined Chucatah himfelf to be the impoftor. What contributed greatly to raife this report, was, that three Mohock Indians were, after making the tour of England and Ireland, made a fhew of in the Strand, and immediately confounded by the public with the Cherokees, and I accufed of making a fhew all over England of Indians who never ftirred out of London. Had I fhowed them, I fhould not have been under fuch anxiety to have them fent away; I fhould have wifhed their ftay, or been able to have fent them back without any inconveniency in raifing the neceffary money for that purpofe: but as it was entirely out of my power, I was advifed to put in an advertifement for a public contribution; I firft, however, refolved to prefent a petition to the Board of Trade, in anfwer to which Lord H——h told me, that it no way concerned

concerned them, but Lord H——, to whom I muſt again apply. On a ſecond application, Lord H——h agreed I ſhould be paid for the time they remained in London, and that he would take care to have them ſent home. I was allowed two guineas a week for the month they ſtayed afterwards in town; but from Mr. Trueheart's death, what in cloaths, paint, trinkets, coach-hire, and other expences, including the bill from their late lodgings (for which I was arreſted, and put to a conſiderable expence) and the time they had lived with me, I had expended near ſeventy pounds, which I muſt enevitably loſe, as Lord H—— has abſolutely refuſed to reimburſe me.

About the beginning of March 1765, by the deſire of Mr. Montague, I accompanied the Indians on board the Madeira packet, in which they returned to their own country, leaving me immerſed in debts not my own, and plunged into difficulties thro' my zeal to ſerve both them and my country, from which the ſelling of twenty pounds a year out of my

com

commiffion has rather allayed than extricated
me. The Indians expreffed the higheft grati-
tude and grief for my misfortunes; all the recompence they could offer, was an afylum in
their country, which I declined; fince their
murmurs, and fome unguarded expreffions
they dropt, convinced me they would not fail
at their return to fpirit up their countrymen,
to vindicate their right by force of arms, which
would infallibly again have been laid to my
charge, and I perhaps be reputed a traitor to
my country. My circumftances, however, are
now fo much on the decline, that when I can
fatisfy my creditors, I muft retire to the Cherokee, or fome other hofpitable country, where
unobferved I and my wife may breathe upon
the little that yet remains.

F I N I S.

A Curious secret Journal tak[en]
——— of a FRENCH

Made in the USA
Lexington, KY
07 August 2018